otter |

Contemporary Film Directors

Edited by James Naremore

The Contemporary Film Directors series provides concise, well-written introductions to directors from around the world and from every level of the film industry. Its chief aims are to broaden our awareness of important artists, to give serious critical attention to their work, and to illustrate the variety and vitality of contemporary cinema. Contributors to the series include an array of internationally respected critics and academics. Each volume contains an incisive critical commentary, an informative interview with the director, and a detailed filmography.

A list of books in the series appears at the end of this book.

Sally Potter |

Catherine Fowler

UNIVERSITY OF ILLINOIS PRESS
URBANA AND CHICAGO

Frontispiece: Sally Potter. © Nicola Dove, Eye Box

Library of Congress Cataloging-in-Publication Data
Fowler, Catherine, 1969–
Sally Potter / Catherine Fowler.
p.   cm. — (Contemporary film directors)
Includes bibliographical references and index.
ISBN 978-0-252-03382-7 (cloth : alk. paper)
ISBN 978-0-252-07576-6 (pbk. : alk. paper)
1. Potter, Sally—Criticism and interpretation.
I. Title.
PN1998.3.P68F69   2008
791.4302'33092—dc22   2008019207

Contents |

Acknowledgments

My interest in Sally Potter's films was engendered in the late 1980s when I first saw *Thriller* for a course on alternative forms in film at Bulmershe College of Higher Education in Reading. For showing me that film and encouraging me in my pursuit of all things alternative, I thank Jim Hillier. The preparation of this book was undertaken thanks to time and money given by the Division of Humanities and the Department of Media, Film, and Communication at Otago University in Dunedin, New Zealand. I would particularly like to thank Dennis Davis for trusting that the book was something I needed to complete and for supporting me in doing so. I would also like to thank David Curtis and Steven Ball at the British Artist's Film and Video Study Collection in London for their help in researching Potter's early career and their prompt answers to questions. Alex Johnson, Mike Manzi, Christopher Sheppard, and I'm sure many others at Adventure Pictures helped by corresponding and finding information and images. James Naremore, anonymous readers, and Joan Catapano at the University of Illinois Press provided invaluable feedback and comments. Finally, in the spirit of Sally Potter's most well-known film, *Orlando,* I would like to dedicate this book to my daughter, Imogen: I hope I can inspire you as you have already inspired me. May you also continue your mother's creative acts.

Expanding Cinema |

At age fourteen, Sally Potter declared to the world by way of her close acquaintances and family that she was going to be a filmmaker. For over thirty years, Potter's precocity has driven her career, which has included the production of five features: *The Gold Diggers* (1983), *Orlando* (1992), *The Tango Lesson* (1997), *The Man Who Cried* (2000), and *YES* (2004); five shorts: *Jerk* (1969), *Black and White* (1969), *Play* (1971), *Thriller* (1979), and *The London Story* (1986); four expanded-cinema works, projected with live performance: *Combines* (1970), *Daily* (1970), *The Building* (1970), *Hors d'oeuvres* (1971); and two documentary projects made for television: *Tears, Laughter, Fears, and Rage* (1986) and *I Am an Ox, I Am a Horse, I Am a Man, I Am a Woman* (1988). In addition to writing and directing, she has also taken on the roles of producer, cameraperson, editor, choreographer, musical director, composer, singer, and even actress.

Potter is primarily known for her adaptation of Virginia Woolf's novel *Orlando*. The success of this film proved Potter's talent and her exemplary independent credentials; *Orlando* was a labor of love that she and her producer, Christopher Sheppard, struggled for seven years to fund and realize. Prior to *Orlando,* Potter's early years were spent making short films that would often be shown during, or as part of, performances. Her first more widely known film, *Thriller,* can be seen as part of an antinarrative, feminist zeitgeist that carried the film to numerous festivals and screenings around the world, from a debut at the Edinburgh Film Festival in 1979 to bookings in Berlin and Chicago. Potter traveled with her film to explain it and orient its reception by theorists and critics. Following the suggestion from the British Film Institute that she develop a feature-length script, Potter made *The Gold Diggers.*

The mostly unfavorable reception of this film, which was seen as overly didactic, made it nearly impossible to raise the money to adapt Woolf's "unadaptable" novel. Once exposed to this early, earnestly feminist, performance-artist side of Potter, we begin to see the tension in *Orlando* between the purely cinematic elements, such as camera movements and sharp editing, and more theatrical effects, including Orlando's reverse looks to camera, set-piece songs, dancing, and the ironic use of well-known performers: Tilda Swinton (theater actress), Heathcote Williams (poet and writer), Quentin Crisp (writer and gay icon), and Jimmy Sommerville (former singer in the British band Bronski Beat).

From *Orlando* onwards, Potter's talent as a dancer, lyricist, and composer are fully evident. She cowrote the score for *Orlando,* danced in *The Tango Lesson,* produced the music for her epic *The Man Who Cried,* and wrote the verse for *YES. The Tango Lesson* was eagerly anticipated; however, instead of being the big-budget follow-up to *Orlando* that some had expected, it was a more personal film. The critical reception was divided: Potter was accused of narcissism for casting herself as the filmmaker who decides to learn the tango and subsequently falls for her teacher. But the story is based on her own experience: in a chapter for the book *Projections 4,* Potter details the long time she spent learning the tango ("Gotta Dance"), and in interviews she has implied that her attraction to her teacher was sublimated in the film. Who else but she could have played that part?

Given the glaring lack of such accusations for male directors who cast themselves in autobiographical films—Woody Allen or Nanni Moretti, for example—this response to *The Tango Lesson* illustrates the unequal ground on which female directors have to build their careers, just as the film itself presents some of the complexities of being a woman "in charge." Despite these recurring accusations, many critics appreciated what Claire Monk characterizes as the "significant risk" that Potter took in appearing in her own film (54). Monk also notes that as an under-marketed director (as are most women directors), "the experience [of appearing in her own film] must have been closer to self-exposure" (54). There was also praise for Potter's mastery of the tango and her metaphoric use of it to critique power relations between the sexes.

Following the success of *Orlando* and the mixed reviews received by *The Tango Lesson*, Potter still could not command the trust of producers, who made her cut over twenty scenes in the week before the shoot for *The Man Who Cried*. The film features a lush, moving soundtrack, and the child's-eye view through which the tale is told serves as a reminder of the exile that most of the characters face. But the film was not as overwhelmingly successful as it might have been and failed to convince as *Orlando* had.

Potter's largest-scale project was followed by a return to her experimental roots. A low-budget poetic drama that began as a five-minute short, *YES* was made with U.K. Film Council funding and with additional investment from the U.S. independent GreeneStreet Films. Audiences were surprised, and critics were divided once more.

This outline of Potter's career shows that she has remained an exemplary independent director who has relentlessly struggled to make only the films she wants to make. She has fought against the prejudices encountered by any film director working in Britain. Male directors such as Derek Jarman, Peter Greenaway, Terence Davies, Stephen Frears, and Michael Winterbottom have all struggled to undertake their craft. Yet this is even more the case for female directors. In the 1970s and 1980s, Laura Mulvey worked with Peter Wollen on several films, all of which intended to put feminist and avant-garde theories into practice. Lezli-Ann Barrett made the one-off *Business as Usual* (1987), starring Glenda Jackson and Cathy Tyson. In the 1990s, Antonia Bird and Beeban Kidron managed to work between the film and television industries, while Carine Adler debuted with the promising *Under the Skin* (1997), and Lynne Ramsay followed critically praised short films with *Ratcatcher* (1999) and *Morvern Callar* (2002). Despite the promise reflected in this list of talented women, all have struggled, and none has achieved a sustained career as a director to the extent that Potter has.

The absence of a prolonged female gaze from behind the camera, so stoically identified by feminist film theory in the 1970s, persists in British cinema. Although Potter's films circulate in an international context where there are more female directors, the lack of an available female role model may be one reason she has looked to literature, dance, and music to find shared interests and creative companions. Another reason for her leaning toward other artistic forms and contexts must be her own artistic origins as a latecomer to dance and a talented musician and performer. Her interests and influences come not only from film but also from fine art (Marcel Duchamp, Robert Rauschenberg, conceptualism, and minimalism), theater (Bertolt Brecht), and literature (Jorge Luis Borges, Colette, Virginia Woolf, James Joyce, John Berger, and Graham Greene on screenwriting).

Potter has also struggled against predictability and safe options. She admires the nonnarrative strategies of those artists named above while she also believes that to involve and engage an audience, one must tell stories. Across Potter's work we see the negotiation of this contradiction, with *Orlando* acknowledged by audiences, critics, and scholars as her most successful effort. Despite the success of *Orlando,* Potter chose to wait until she could make a project she wanted rather than take up the many offers of director-for-hire. Her struggles have paid off, as her films consistently challenge and delight audiences across the world. It seems only right, given the fighting spirit with which Potter has approached her calling, that those who watch and study her films should do battle with their preconceived notions of what cinema can and should be. This book argues that the significance of Potter's vision arises from the way in which it connects cinema with literature, theater, dance, and music, challenging our understanding of the boundaries that cinema shares with the other arts. In other words, Potter has always been intent on creating something that is an "expansion" of cinema.

In the penultimate sequence of *YES*, the main couple embrace on a beach. They are known only as SHE, a scientist with Northern Irish roots, and HE, a doctor from Lebanon working as a chef in London. They kiss, and the digital effects slow this gesture down so that their faces cross over and merge, becoming streaks of color. As film endings go, this image is relatively unremarkable; a couple coming together is the paradigmatic concluding moment of many films. However, in Potter's work this ending is extremely uncharacteristic; although all of her films close with her female protagonist in the frame, her women are never so harmoniously "coupled." In *The Man Who Cried,* Suzie/Fegele finally finds the father she thought was lost and returns to him the lullaby he had once sung to her to help her to sleep. In *The Tango Lesson,* Pablo has admitted to being afraid of being someone without roots who might simply disappear without leaving a trace; in response, Sally sings to him, they dance and kiss, but they are still far from resolving their differences. Although men *and* women occupy the final frame in these films, the coming together is either emotional and filial or awkward.

In Potter's other films, the women either end the film alone (*Thriller*) or with another woman (*The Gold Diggers,* where Celeste has rescued Ruby; or *Orlando,* where Orlando stands under a [family] tree with her video-making daughter). Although at some point in these narratives the women (Mimi, Ruby, and Orlando) are in relationships with men, they remain unfulfilled, wanting more for themselves and feeling that there must be more to life, just as Potter seems to feel that there must be more to narrative cinema than the coming together of the couple.

How can we read this refusal in Potter's films to matchmake? First, the deletion of the romantic imperative leaves her narratives open to a diverse range of meaningful connections. Removing the onus on coupling has several effects: it frees up the actions of the female protagonists, allows movement within power relationships, lets the spotlight fall on female friendships, and permits the male figures more breadth. Consequently, the dynamics of power and pleasure are vastly different. Instead of the quest to find a romantic partner that drives many cause-and-effect narratives, Potter's characters seek answers to questions about their sexual, gender, social, cultural, and ethnic identities. They find answers by retelling stories, investigating mysteries, traveling, and interacting with people. These different quests do not necessarily reduce their destiny to that of finding a matching half.

Second, the deletion of the romantic imperative makes for stories that offer unexpected pleasures, since the narrative line becomes only one trajectory in films that communicate through music—opera in *Thriller* and *The Man Who Cried* and lush soundtracks in other films;

choreographed movements and dance in *Thriller, The Tango Lesson,* and *Orlando;* and heightened or poetic dialogue in *Orlando* and *YES.* Potter's cinema gives us sound and image at their fullest because it is allied to the other arts from which it takes techniques and ideas. This abundance of sound and image infects her female characters, who also burst with life and all its possibilities.

A further area that is opened up through the downgrading of romance is identity, which can be explored in ethnic, racial, religious, cultural, class, and sexual terms. In Potter's early featurette *Thriller,* it is clear that the battle of the sexes is only one axis of oppression that Mimi has to cope with. Feminism and postfeminism have been accused of creating subjects that are purely white, western, middle-class and heterosexual (Projansky). Even though Potter's work has engaged with both feminist and postfeminist discourses, it can be distinguished by its conviction that gender is not the only reason for the oppression of women, a reflection of Potter's own involvement in liberation politics. The creation of something that is "more than cinema" delivers new options for her women and a unique combination of creative opportunities.

The "more" that Potter's female characters desire is aptly summarized by the narrator at the start of *Orlando.* In our introduction to Orlando, who paces under an oak tree trying to memorize verse he will recite for the (shortly arriving) Queen Elizabeth I, we are told that despite having heritage and privilege, what he seeks (and therefore will seek throughout the film) is "company." The irony of this opening would seem to be that while seeking company, in also wanting to be a writer Orlando must, of necessity, be alone. This creativity/company dialectic extends across Potter's work; it represents the conflict faced by all her heroines. Mimi, Celeste and Ruby, Orlando, Sally, Suzie, and SHE are all caught between being true to themselves and following their own paths or entering into friendships and relationships that become power struggles. This notion of creativity comes to stand for trying to find a place for oneself in narrative.

Potter's early films play with well-known, "found" narratives. In *Thriller,* Giacomo Puccini's opera *La Bohème* and Alfred Hitchcock's film *Psycho* are the intertexts, and once narrative expression fails, music, dance, choreography, and effects of the image take over. The tipping of the balance from conventional communication strategies such as narrative and dialogue towards other creative alternatives such as dance, singing, and music is graphically played out in *The Man Who Cried,* in which Fegele has a forced assimilation, losing her original language but finding her singing voice.

Each of Potter's main characters wants to interact with the world, to be able to move around it freely, to act on their desires, to live and work as they wish, and to be understood and respected. And each character meets with barriers that prevent this. Mimi is born a lowly seamstress, and her poverty brings her ill health. Ruby is trapped by her past and unable to think for herself. Orlando finds him/herself subject to the social restrictions of inheritance and birthright, while Sally encounters only misapprehension about her creative and sexual desires. Suzie meets with prejudice against her Jewish background, and SHE is trying to find the right environment in which she can embrace her desires free from anyone else's views on them.

At the heart of Potter's work we find a concern with the ways in which narrative circumscribes the actions of women, their ability to act, speak, look, desire, and think for themselves. Her first two films deconstruct found stories, clichés, and conventional images. The films that follow create new and original narratives that place female acts, voices, looks, desires, and thoughts at their center. In order to achieve this, Potter frees her camera and her mise-en-scène and editing strategies from the patriarchal attitudes of conventional cinema. Her women exist unobjectified and unfetishized; they are never filmed nude (except for one key moment in *Orlando*) and when they are subject to a male gaze from within the story world—for example, Orlando's look at Sacha, Pablo's at Sally, César's at Suzie, or HIS at HER, it should be evident that these are highly complex gazes. Not only is the assumed power of the looker problematic, but these gazes are not controlling in nature. Each is part of a carefully sketched matrix of power and its lack, which is bound up with the character's social, cultural, ethnic, and sexual identity. Objectification of the female characters is also discouraged by their role as observers through whom we experience the narrative. Potter's women, whether as characters or spectators, simply have more options, and her men, though they may begin as archetypes, become increasingly complex figures.

The "more" that Potter's creativity gives to her films can be seen in the multiple roles she often assumes, from undertaking everything but the acting in *Thriller,* to writing, directing, composing, singing, choreographing, and starring in *The Tango Lesson.* Potter's background as a performance artist has shaped her interest in anti-illusionist tactics. The modernist literature of Virginia Woolf and James Joyce, the revolutionary montage techniques of the Russian directors Sergei Eisenstein and Vsevolod Pudovkin, and the playfulness of Marx brothers comedies have also been important influences.

Unsurprisingly, given these sources, the singular narrative that travels from A (problem set up) to B (problem solved) has always been too limiting for Potter. Her narratives get distracted by the desire to include theatrical elements, play and comedy, dance, song, and choreographed movement. She also incorporates figures that use looks and/or words to comment on the action, inviting us to reflect, critique, or even laugh with them. She uses every expressive register at her disposal—her expertise and talent as a dancer, performer, musician, and lyricist—to make meaning on the screen. Consequently, Potter's cinema expresses itself at the meeting of visual, verbal, and aural languages. Different films have emphasized different combinations. In *Thriller* and *YES,* the verbal is highly important, as the former retells a story, weaving feminist deconstruction to reveal the sexual and class politics that are hidden by the tragedy, while in the latter, rhyming couplets allow a blending of the abstract and concrete that is taken up by the images themselves. In *The Tango Lesson* and *The Man Who Cried,* the aural dominates through plots that revolve around music and the physical or emotional response to it. In *The Gold Diggers* and *Orlando* the visual is emphasized through pointed camera movements that comment on relationships between characters and between character and setting. This extrapolation of emphases is not meant to suggest that in any of these films the other languages are not important but simply that each film explores a distinctive combination that serves its narrative and themes and becomes the dominant memory of the film.

Another way in which Potter's cinema gives us more is through the use of performers as well as actors and performances alongside characterizations. Colette Laffont, Rose English, Quentin Crisp, Jimmy Sommerville, Heathcote Williams, and Potter herself appear dialectically in her films, as themselves and as figures with narrative roles. Potter includes the audience by having her characters look directly at us. The commentaries we are given by Orlando and the cleaner in *YES* operate through reverse looks. Typically, a look directly at the camera would be off-limits to fictional narrative, since it would break the illusion of realism. Potter's use of the reverse look accompanies her use of music as a way in which she can draw in her audience, pulling them beyond passive involvement.

The outstanding success of *Orlando* has largely overshadowed assessment of Potter's short films and early work as a performer. Due to the inconsistent coverage of her films since *Orlando,* attempts to read across her work have been limited; each film has typically been read in isolation. Although each of Potter's feature films have been distinctive, they share themes, preoccupations, and stylistic features that make a study of her entire work a worthwhile task.

These breaches and inconsistencies in the critical reception of Potter's oeuvre have left particular gaps for this book to fill. First, dealing with Potter's early career, the importance of performance art is emphasized, the live experience and the collaborations that she would take from this arena into her filmmaking. As a consequence, the "postgender" politics and parodic style in *Orlando,* which are typically viewed by critics as evidence of a postmodern sensibility, can be reread as part of her 1970s performance persona and early concerns. The first section of this book will examine Potter's early work as a performance artist, dancer, and singer, her multimedia work with film and performers, and her early films made in the context of the emergence of the London Filmmakers Co-op and expanded cinema.

The following section explores the moment that Potter became a filmmaker through the explicit act of stepping from in front of to behind the camera. This moment is likened to Virginia Woolf's notion of a writer needing a "room of one's own." The distinctive creative signature strongly evident in *Orlando* is rarely connected to the work that precedes it, in which Potter rehearses the birth of "Potter" in particular and women in general as creators. In this work she carefully considers the attendant power play associated with the acts of finding a space of one's own to write, taking charge of narrative, and controlling the frame and those bodies that live within it. She also negotiates the contradiction between her nonnarrative interests and her desire to tell stories. This examination of Potter's leap from writer and performer to director tells us much about the complexities of authorship for a female director based in Britain who is determined to retain her independence, yet who also listens to and learns from her audience. This section focuses on two definitive stylistic elements of Potter's work: first, her camera work and editing, both of which develop a playful attitude to her performers and characters, and second, her use of the reverse look, to involve us.

Once Potter's early years are considered, more sense can be made of the shape her oeuvre has taken, through noting her key concerns and her developing individual style and obsessions in her first two films, *Thriller* and *The Gold Diggers*. Recurrent themes and issues, such as how women might tell their own stories and how narrative might be altered by the female look and voice and broadened to include pleasures provided by the other arts, will be introduced. Both films remain experimental, yet their combination of still and moving images, choreographed performance, and music feeds into the more popular work to come. These films abandon classical narrative; instead, meaning is made through deconstruction and juxtaposition and the layering of themes and spaces. Both films offer complex experiences that in many ways go against Potter's stated wish to give pleasure. This paradox is examined in detail, with the conclusion that *The Gold Diggers* constitutes the end of Potter's antinarrative, anti-illusionist phase. *Orlando* therefore becomes the bridge between Potter's avant-garde work and the more commercially aware art cinema of her last three films.

Orlando and *the Tango Lesson* will be compared in terms of their examination of male and female desire, their episodic narratives, and their development of the company/creativity dialectic. In *Orlando,* although illusionism is present, key narrative moments are undercut by conspicuous camera movement or brusque editing. Orlando's reverse looks connect us to these parodic and theatrical worlds. In *The Tango Lesson,* Sally's desiring gaze at Pablo suggests the simultaneous creation of an idea and an attraction. In acting on that desire, Sally has to negotiate male narcissism and a form of femininity that she has previously been happy to reject because of its associations with powerlessness. If Orlando escapes her past by being given a gift from the future (her daughter and a video camera), then Sally overcomes her fears by separating Sally/dancer from Sally/director and creating with Pablo, but dancing with others.

In Potter's most recent films, *The Man Who Cried* and *YES*, the male characters finally achieve a complexity missing from her early work. As a result, the women also have more options. *The Man Who Cried* examines exile and displacement against the backdrop of an opera company in pre–World War II Europe; though its scope is large, its focus is intimate. The main character, Suzie, is an exiled Russian Jew who takes up Potter's familiar position of observer. Through Suzie's eyes we see how a variety of characters cope with exile, as well as how ideas of home and identity are complicated by gypsy characters and those turning their backs on the past. The setting for *YES* is the contemporary, post-9/11 world. Several of Potter's key themes return in this film, including the need to put difference aside and the difficulty of achieving equality in relationships. These themes are given an experimental twist by camera work that shifts focus, sound that is exaggerated, and scenes that dissolve into each other. The result is a play with perspective that reinforces the message of *The Gold Diggers* twenty-two years earlier: "Even as I look and even as I see I am changing what is there."

This book closes with some thoughts on the endings of Potter's films. Given their questioning, questing structures, closure is difficult and even undesirable. While resisting the conventions of a happy ending in which all problems are resolved, in different ways Potter's endings constitute a move forward to new relationships, new understandings, and new identities.

London in the 1970s: Performance On- and Offscreen

She may have traveled with her films to the far corners of the earth, but Sally Potter has remained based in London, where she was born Charlotte Sally Potter on September 19, 1949. Two characteristics of her cinema can be seen to have been encouraged by her upbringing. First, she grew up in an atheist and anarchist background, where there was a tendency to ask rather than answer questions. The issue-based nature of films such as *The Gold Diggers* and *YES* is clearly informed by these early years. Potter has managed to impose a great deal of order on what could have been a fairly chaotic view of the world. Second, strong artistic, musical, and acting influences in her family exposed her to the attractions of the arts for individual expression from an early age. Both grandmothers were actresses, and she has recalled writing plays at age ten and putting on shows at eleven (MacDonald, "Interview" 192).

With home as well as school the sites of learning, Potter first picked up a camera at fourteen (lent to her by her uncle); she left school at sixteen with the intention of teaching herself to direct films. Her blinkered determination did not stop her from exploring other creative routes, and though she joined the London Filmmakers' Co-op and was eagerly going to screenings of experimental work and hanging out at the Arts Lab, she also took courses in fine art and dance. About a yearlong foundation course at St. Martin's School of Art, she has said: "What I got from it above all was life drawing, a sense of draftsmanship and composition within the frame, which has been a passionate engagement ever since" (MacDonald, "Interview" 197). About her viewing habits at this time, she has remarked: "In my teens, I went to film societies and gobbled up Eisenstein and the Russians, and a lot of early cinema. By the time I was seventeen I was watching anything the Filmmakers' Co-op had, from Warhol's stuff to *Wavelength* [dir. Michael Snow, 1967]. . . . And I loved Godard and Truffaut. . . . I gobbled up whatever there was" (MacDonald, "Interview" 193). These experimental tastes were later mixed with more mainstream obsessions, from Charlie Chaplin and Alfred Hitchcock to Michael Powell, Ealing comedies, and the Marx brothers.

Potter joined the Arts Lab (1968–70) and the London Filmmakers' Co-op and made *Jerk*, which featured another director, Mike Dunford. She also worked with Dunford on one part of his *Four Films* (1971). While showing *Jerk* at festivals and using the facilities of the Filmmakers' Co-op, Potter also enrolled in classes in dance and choreography at The Place (1971–74). At age twenty-one, she was a late starter as a dancer, and she has lamented this as one possible reason that she never reached the expert heights that she would have liked. What she learned at the school accustomed her to the physical work and mental concentration that she was able to deliver even at forty-eight, as a tango novice. While learning dance, she made her next short films, *Black and White* and *Play,* and put together four expanded-cinema works, *Combines, The Building, Daily,* and *Hors d'oeuvres,* in which dancers and/or choreographed bodies feature heavily. The performances that Potter would be involved in during the 1970s as a dancer, choreographer, musician, and performance artist, in keeping with the modernist bent of the late 1960s and early 1970s, were non-illusionist and explored the role of the performer and the audience in a performance. The notion of performance as an exchange and act of communication between both ends may seem at odds with the finished and closed nature of filmmaking. However, Potter has always retained this as a desirable model, and wherever possible she has generated dialogue offscreen by traveling extensively with her films. Most recently, she has kept a detailed Web diary to accompany her round-the-world screenings of *YES* (see www.sallypotter.com). Onscreen she has generated dialogue by foregrounding performances within her narratives, using music and dance and including observer figures who give whispered asides to the audience.

The dance and film worlds in the 1970s shared a poststructuralist distrust of language, which led to performances and films intent on taking language apart rather than on making meaning. In North America this tendency produced performance art by practitioners such as Yoko Ono, Carolee Schneeman, Robert Morris, Laurie Anderson, Vito Acconci, Dan Graham, and Yvonne Rainer. Rainer is perhaps the closest of this group to Potter, since she too moved from dance performances to cinema. As part of the Judson Dance Theater in 1962, she created performances in which the dancer's body was no longer circumscribed by the turned-out, stylized, and unnatural movements of ballet. Instead, bodies were allowed to move in performance as one would move every day. This kind of dance mixed the choreographed and practiced with the quotidian in a bid to do away with dance's previous "emphasis on nuance and skilled accomplishment, its accessibility to comparison and interpretation, its involvement with connoisseurship, its introversion, narcissism and self-congratulatoriness"; bodies were allowed to "stand, walk, run, eat, carry bricks" (Rainer 65). Having broken dance down into "[the] understanding of bodies in time and space, and . . . the movement vocabulary that emerged from close contact with other bodies" (Goldberg 18), Rainer added the vocabulary of film to her work, before turning exclusively to film.

In Britain, performance work was also proliferating, and Potter's contemporaries included Rose Garrard, Annabel Nicholson, Rose English, Sylvia Ziranek, Bobby Baker, Tina Keane, Catherine Elwes, Mary Kelly, and Roberta Graham. This list of names indicates the importance of performance art for women artists. These women created work in which their female bodies acknowledged their status as objects of the look and commented on, challenged, or problematized that status. They used fragmentary narratives or a mixed collage of elements and tested the audience at every turn. The boundaries between dance and film were bridged in multimedia performance art or, in the cinematic context, expanded cinema. Potter's output hovered between these two worlds, although at this early stage she had more connections with dancers than filmmakers. She once said that she has "always felt like a loner, an outsider. I never felt part of a community of filmmakers. I was often the only female, or one of few" (MacDonald, "Interview" 192).

Potter's early work experimented with mixed-media possibilities. *Black and White* and *Play* were made to be projected onto two screens. *Combines, The Building,* and *Daily* (all made in 1970) mixed multi-screen footage with live performers. *Play* was a two-screen film, and *Hors d'oeuvres,* like *Jerk,* was single-screen. Her mixed-media performances can be seen as examples of the opening up of the languages of film and dance so that both become "live," and the bodies on- and offscreen take on extra connotations. However, they also inevitably suffer from the problem of transience associated with all live work. Footage still exists for some of these films and performances, while for others even Potter's memory has faded.

Accounts of those films that no longer exist suggest that each places the filmed in direct relation to and rubbing up against the live. Of *Black and White,* Potter has simply said, "[P]eople push against the edge of the frame" (MacDonald, "Interview" 193), and of *Daily,*

> Each performer was filmed in his or her home doing something that they did every day (making a bed, tidying a room, etc.). Each film is projected three times, shown on double screens, in various combinations. During the first iteration, performers enter and stand still, while tape plays of them discussing their actions on film. During the second iteration each performer mimes, in exact synchronization with his or her image on film, and during the third iteration the mime is simplified or abstracted. Finally, each performer enacts his or her own movements without film to connect with others. (www.sallypotter.com; accessed April 25, 2008)

The past tense of the moving image, representing actions that "have been done," is combined with the present unfolding of the dancers' actions in front of the screen. Bodies onscreen and onstage are compared and contrasted, and the experience of watching a film and watching a live performance underlines the differences in language and perception of each. This mixing of languages is combined with a mixing of exhibition spaces, as Potter's works at this time were shown in dance spaces and cinemas.

This mixing of the dance, performance, and film worlds created hybrid forms, but there were other practices in Britain at this time that we can juxtapose with Potter's. *The Building* in particular can be compared to the expanded cinema that was coming out of the London Filmmakers' Co-op around this time, even though this was not a scene that Potter was wholly involved in. While much experimental cinema attacked illusionism from within the confines of the cinematic frame, expanded cinema extended this attack to the auditorium itself, disturbing the black-box ideal of projection and forcing its audience to reflect on the cinematic apparatus in the broadest sense.

The term "expanded cinema" has been used to encompass the work of Lis Rhodes, Gill Eatherley, Annabel Nicholson, Anthony McCall, and Malcolm Le Grice, among others. For the women in this group, multiple-screen projection events often included a feminist element. Gill Eatherley's *Aperture Sweep* (1973) consists of her sweeping the white screen with a broom wired up to a microphone; halfway through, a projected shadow appears on one side, also sweeping, and she interacts with it. In Annabel Nicholson's *Reel Time* (1973), she sits facing the audience with the film going through the projector then through her sewing machine and back through the projector, while a second projector casts her shadow onto the screen. Both pieces seem designed to comment ironically on those actions considered as women's work and fit easily alongside the feminist documentaries of the time. By contrast, Malcolm Le Grice's *Horror Film 1* (1971) features him topless, standing in front of the screen, making "horrific" shadows through the projector's beam: the materiality of the live body and its projected shadowy presence is the focus. Expanding the cinema space from audience and screen to audience, screen, and performer was his and others' way of creating a dialectical image that compelled the audience to think about the material of film and how the processes of perception of this medium worked.

Potter's performances have slightly different intentions from these expanded-cinema pieces, as evidenced in an account of *The Building*, performed by Mike Dunford and Letha Papaconstantinou:

> It started with a man and a woman dressed in white sitting with their backs to the audience on the stage in front of two screens. On the screens there appeared in negative their own images getting ready for the show. It showed them coming into a white area and sitting down on black chairs with their backs to the audience. The sound track consisted at this stage of half-words, which reflected the small half-movements the characters made. Eventually they took off their baggy white costumes and revealed red satin skin-tight clothing with exaggerated padding, so that the woman was exaggeratedly feminine, and the man had great padded shoulders. They looked at themselves in two mirrors and began taking up exaggerated poses, which finally tore their clothes until they were standing in rags. . . . [I]t ended with the films showing their images crossing and recrossing from screen to screen and laughing. (Glaessner, "Interviews" 46)

This account suggests not simply Potter's attack on the conventions of theater and cinema but also her feminist intent, creating exaggerated gender divisions in her performers. We can add to this example *Combines*, a piece made in collaboration with the choreographer Richard Alston for the London Contemporary Dance Theatre. (Potter joined Alston's Strider dance company in 1971 as a dancer and choreographer.) As Scott MacDonald describes it, "*Combines* used three, contiguously mounted screens to present seven separate sequences, most with musical accompaniment. These sequences—sometimes using one of the three screens, sometimes two, and in a single instance all three—introduced the live dance company, provided five entr'actes, plus a conclusion that accompanied the audience's exit from the theatre" ("Interview" 188).

The more well known and documented expanded-cinema work of Le Grice, Eatherley, Nicholson, and others aimed to explore the physicality of film and the film-projecting equipment. The body of the artist was therefore used, in all cases, to produce this emphasis, as physical presence made the projection into a live experience. Despite the use of live bodies, expanded-cinema makers were not really interested in the bodies themselves. For Potter, the bodies, since they were those of dancers, were extremely important and emphasized the fact that the movement of the cinematic images was to be matched, compared, and contrasted to the movement of the live bodies in front of the screens. The frame was also to be used self-consciously by Potter, who had been a member of a "happenings" group called Group Events in the late 1960s. One of their preoccupations was to break the theatrical frame through nontheatrical performances. Despite the formalism of her work, even at this stage there was some evidence of narrative, or at least the possibility of a storytelling function, which is completely eradicated in expanded-cinema.

The footage that accompanied Potter's performances explored the differences between on- and offscreen performance. Potter has said that technical problems led her to abandon expanded-cinema/performance work: "[I]t was just so unsatisfactory . . . if you had enough light to show the performers, it was spilling onto the screen. If projectors were in the room, they broke down, you couldn't synchronize them properly" (interview with the author, August 18, 2004). Turning from these performance pieces to her films, what becomes evident is the complete lack of illusionism and her interest in how framing and editing might choreograph the body's movement in a different way; we might see Eisenstein in the background of these interests. In a grant application submitted in 1973, Potter states her interest in "analys[ing] the nature of formalized movement (dance) and the nature of recording or containing movement in time (film)" (Potter, "There Will"). *Play* and *Hors d'oeuvres* further this exploration. The first focuses on the control that a camera may or may not be able to exercise over moving bodies when it frames them and of the manipulation of live action through postproduction techniques. *Play* uses two cameras to film three pairs of twins (MacDonald, "Interview" 187) from a second-story window as they play on the pavement below.

The foreground of the frame is dominated by a horizontal bar, probably a railing, on which the children occasionally lean. The high angle and static camera also sometimes cuts heads and parts of bodies out of the frame. What could have been a candid-camera look at the uninhibited interactions of children is transformed through the game that Potter plays with the footage, which was edited in-camera. First, the two-camera setup is matched by a two-screen, expanded-cinema projection that creates a dividing line in the middle of the action. The left-hand screen is in color, while the right-hand screen is in black and

Play experiments with split screen.
© Adventure Pictures Ltd.

white, further dividing the action. There is a spatial ellipsis at the point where the two cameras meet, so that action traveling from left to right does not immediately appear on the right-hand screen.

At times the children simply play with each other as if ignorant of the camera—a boy pushes another on a tricycle, a girl grabs the other by the elbow and they whirl around. However, the high angle of the camera and the railings set up the space as a stage on which the children perform; therefore, at other times the children do seem aware of the camera, and they often turn towards it and lean over the bar as if trying to see the audience. Whether these children are actually playing or whether they have been encouraged to act up is unclear. The discontinuity of action across screens is matched by a series of effects on each side. At one point, a black woman walks across the left-hand screen carrying a bag. Her hurrying gait is slowed down, and then the shot is immediately repeated twice more before she appears on the right-hand screen.

Comparing *Play* to other British two-screen work at the time, we can see that it shares a preoccupation with creating a comparative experience. Once again, though, there is more evidence of narrative elements and an interest in bodies and their movement under certain conditions. Potter expresses this thus: "I was beginning to ask the question, which other people in the Co-op at this time were not, what is performance on film?" (MacDonald, "Interview" 193). It is emphatically the human presence in the frame that Potter manipulates. *Play* is less about the camera than the subject. Although Verina Glaessner suggested in 1973 that Potter is interested in "using the structural form to deal with specific subjects within a revolutionary context" (Glaessner, "Sally Potter" 8), Potter can be seen as avant-garde in her inclusive approach to film language (not excluding the power of dance and music) and her analytical intent, yet she was always committed to exploring a narrative experience. This concern is revealed in interviews where she repeats her desire to please her audience, not by offering a "lowest common denominator" experience but by offering a hook, something familiar that will guide them through an otherwise unfamiliar and complex experience.

The final short film that precedes and can be seen as research for *Thriller* is *Hors d'oeuvres*. Verina Glaessner documents a version she saw in 1972: "It attempts to relate the token physicality of the dance to the technical sophistication of the film . . . poses figures, bodies in relation to defined space, to a room and a hard-edged window, and explores the relationship of the bodies in their rhythmic slow dance movements to the angular static form of the space that encloses them" (Glaessner, "Sally Potter" 8). Glaessner also mentions Potter's intention to add a sound track.

The footage that still exists is silent and is largely consonant with Glaessner's description. In common with Potter's other shorts, an exploration of bodies in space is emphasized, although here the dancers who had previously performed live in front of her footage find their place onscreen. The footage begins in color and then switches to black and white. Throughout the film the image is heavily degraded and sometimes even looks like animation. Potter describes the process she went through to attain this effect:

> I shot on 8mm color film and projected it onto a ground glass screen and made a black and white 8mm film of that, and then I made a negative from the positive so that I ended up with three films. Then using two projectors, one loaded with the black and white positive, I projected them onto the screen and filmed them on 16 alternately, stopping and starting the projectors. I did the same with the black and white positive and with the color film, again with two projectors. And there's an 8mm film of close-ups of the original. (Glaessner, "Interviews" 46)

Unlike in her previous films, where we find a mix of choreography and daily actions, it is largely balletic poses that are struck by several of the male and female bodies that appear in the room. The room itself is a divided space, thus as we concentrate on a body in the foreground, much of the rest of the space is often masked or irised off, or at times bodies moving are revealed by a sweeping spotlight. A woman on the left places her arms in first position; she sweeps round towards us and we are given a double image of her. These effects are repeated on further dancers who are frozen into poses or stopped at the beginning or end of movements. Movements are interrupted, or the middle part of them is elided. Ultimately, this film explores what can be lost or gained by filming dance movement. In the fight for dominance, the camera and editing table have won over the body, which is cut up, duplicated, irised off, and made to repeat and jump cut to elide stages of movement.

Hors d'oeuvres suggests what *Thriller* might have been like had Potter not turned more and more to cinema for her frame of reference. A 1977 Arts Council application for money sets out a quite different kind of film than what emerged as the finished product. Stating that she already possessed filmed performances of choreographed scenes by four performers and "one hundred stills yet to be filmed using a rostrum camera," she states her intention to include "information about the performers' real lives. So far I have filmed two hundred interviews for this section and recorded about four hours tape of the performers talking about performing and about the struggles in their lives that relate to film" (Potter, "Application"). The finished film has cut all of this "self-reflexive" documentary interview footage that gives a sense of the performers' realities. The performers simply play characters from the opera and do not really exist outside of these roles, notwithstanding the fact that there is at times some comedy in how they relate to Colette.

Despite making films filled with increasingly recognizable cinematic conventions, Potter continued to integrate the effects of her live performance and two-screen work: breaking the frame, invading the audience's space, and invoking a performative use of film language. Once we turn to *Thriller,* it is evident that what had taken place in front of the screen found its place onscreen. The body became something enframed and later enplotted, yet its function was still to turn a spotlight on the invisible.

The six-year gap between *Hors d'oeuvres* and *Thriller* was filled with a variety of collaborative and touring work across Britain and America. Those Potter worked with as a performer also became her early collaborators in the transition from dancing and singing to directing, which may explain why *Thriller* and *The Gold Diggers* share so much in common with her performances. Following her work with Richard Alston's Strider dance company (Richard Alston choreographed *Combines*), she cofounded the Limited Dance Company in 1974 with Jacky Lansley; they performed as a duo and with other collaborators. Lansley has remained a dancer; she later played the tap dancer in *The Gold Diggers* who hurries Ruby along while musing to herself on why exactly she has trouble dancing solo. She would also appear as the woman called Jack in *The London Story* and undertake choreography for *Orlando* and *The Man Who Cried.*

Another lasting collaboration was with the performance artist Rose English. English, Potter, and Lansley worked together on large-scale theatrical presentations, including *Death and the Maiden* (1975), and Potter and English collaborated on *Berlin* (1976), a performance in four parts or episodes during which Potter, topless with a skirt of leaves around her waist, skates around a fire on an ice rink. English and Potter also created the musical Feminist Improvising Group (FIG) and the performance piece *Mounting* (1977). English appears as Musetta in *Thriller,* and she would cowrite and be artistic director for *The Gold Diggers.* Her direct involvement with Potter's films ends with *The Gold Diggers,* after which she emerged as one of the most consistently brilliant performance artists in Britain. English's performances create collages of images and sounds, from *Plato's Chair* (1984) to *Walks on Water* (1988). Although she chose a different medium than Potter, her performances contain elements familiar from their early work together. Gender is dissected, and romantic love is challenged. Interestingly, a couple of years after *Orlando,* English created *Tantamount Esperance* (1994), in which she appeared dressed as a man, suggesting some of the shared territory that still exists between the two.

Another key collaborator was Lindsay Cooper. Potter joined her Film Music Orchestra and toured Europe with it as a singer over a four-year period. Potter later worked with Cooper as a lyricist and singer as part of the Marx Brothers group with Georgie Born and the Film Music Orchestra. Potter collaborated (as a singer-songwriter) with Cooper on the song cycle *Oh Moscow,* which was performed throughout Europe, Russia, and North America. Potter, Cooper, and English developed the idea of an opera into *The Gold Diggers,* and Cooper is credited with playing the bassoon on the sound track to *Orlando.*

Potter took this ethic of collaboration forward into her feature films. The low-budget nature of *Thriller* meant that Potter undertook most of the offscreen tasks herself, while onscreen improvisation with the dancers/actors and Colette was used. *The Gold Diggers* has been described as a three-way process between Potter, English, and Cooper; George Yiasoumi and Lol Coxhill both take cameo roles that they have reprised in all of Potter's work to date. *Orlando* defines the break between Potter's collaboration with performers and her work with those whose background had been in the cinema. Her cinematic compatriots are her producer on all her films through the production company Adventure Pictures, Christopher Sheppard; the story editor Walter Donohue (*Orlando, The Tango Lesson, The Man Who Cried, YES*); the cinematographer Alexei Rodionov (*Orlando, YES*); the editor Hervé Schneid (*Orlando, The Tango Lesson, The Man Who Cried*); the costume designer Carlos Conti (*The Tango Lesson, The Man Who Cried, YES*); and Fred Frith, a musician who contributed to *Orlando, The Tango Lesson, The Man Who Cried,* and *YES*.

This formative period contains many of the seeds of Potter's feature-length work. These early films clearly show how much her features would be informed by her past in the theater and on the performance scene. Of equal importance is her apparent inability to choose between creative forms in her early days, which would lead to her all-encompassing approach and would necessitate her creation of something that goes beyond our understanding of—and therefore expands—cinema.

Power Plays: Potter's Search for a "Frame of Her Own"

Potter's background in the arts continues to inform her filmmaking, but there are also moments in her early short films when she confronts the specificities of film language and therefore begins to rehearse the birth of Potter the filmmaker. As a well-read and thoughtful practitioner, it is no surprise that even at the crucial moment that she crosses the line from in front of to behind the camera/audience, she offers insight into the challenges of such a move. First, we must take into account her experience as a performer with breaking the frame through events in the streets or theatrical performances that directly address the audience—the cinematic frame is therefore situated as a point of tension for her. Second, we can see how the influence of dadaist, futurist, and structuralist artists adds a self-conscious inflection to the bodies and figures she frames, as well as the diegetic space and how it is created. Third, there is her passion for Brechtian theories of alienation and the comedy of figures such as the Marx brothers or studios such as Ealing. Together, these interests create the wish to move her audience passionately and politically and create laughter and pleasure through "being with" a film. Potter's feature films (including *Thriller*) are testaments to the difficult ambitions created by her interests and other roles as much as they are examples of the difficulty of women finding a room of their own. By comparing her first film, *Jerk*, with a short film she appeared in at the same time, Potter's opening treatment of the frame, the cut, the camera, and the actor can be seen, as can her acute awareness of the power involved in assuming the role of director.

Potter's adaptation of *Orlando* has been praised for its "cinematic" translation of Woolf's literary style and conceits (Ehrenstein, "Out of the Wilderness" 5; Indiana 88). However, one particular scene from the novel does not appear in the film: that of the extensively described writing process that follows Shelmerdine's departure. In Woolf's novel, when Shelmerdine leaves, "Orlando went indoors. It was completely still, it was very silent. There was the inkpot: there was the pen; there was the manuscript of her poem, broke off in the middle of a tribute to eternity" (182). Orlando begins to write, and Woolf suggests that the lifting of her writer's block is dependent on both her newly married status and her husband's absence. Creativity—something that Orlando has desired throughout the book but has been thwarted due to lack of talent, time, or social access to the means to explore it—is now granted, thanks to the lack of "company."

In Potter's film there is no such scene. Shelmerdine leaves, riding off into the mist once again. We cut to a close-up of Orlando's face, then a wider shot of her as it begins to rain. She shuts her eyes, and when she opens them again airplanes are overhead, and we have once again jumped across centuries to the Second World War. Heavily pregnant, she runs across a muddy battlefield, then we cut to her publisher's office as he drops a hefty manuscript on his desk. This sequence of images makes a correlation between the baby and the book, but otherwise the actual "work" of production that brought about the book, so crucial in Woolf's novel, is elided.

To some extent, the sentiments of Woolf's scene are taken up in Potter's opening scene: both dramatize a conflict between company and creativity, or between finding, in Woolf's words, "a room of one's own" and spending time with companions. We encounter this conflict more than once in Potter's cinema. Swiftly following *Orlando, The Tango Lesson* begins with a blank screen—this time a white table that Potter as "Sally" is intent on cleaning (as if to free herself from her past, like Orlando). Then she sits on a stool and has her pencil poised to write. We are subject to her thoughts as flashes of color in this otherwise black and white world. However, these colorful images are brief, and the pencil writes only one word—"Rage," a title perhaps. Unable to create in solitude, Sally instead seeks company, and we cut to a shot of traffic passing as she is now outside, walking along the street. The street sounds are gradually drowned out by tango music, and the camera tracks alongside her. She stops walking and turns away from the camera to go through a door. The key dialectic between creativity, which one must normally undertake on one's own, and company, which would ordinarily take one away from creating, is set up and aligned with the twin spaces of the empty room (and blank canvas) and the city streets and entertainment to be found there. Hence, this also becomes a mind-versus-body split.

The Tango Lesson, with its director starring as a film director, its narrative that opens with the beginning of the creative process, and its contemplation of the power relations that the look from behind the camera might involve, is an exemplary film for this theme of creativity. But the creativity/company dialectic can also stand in for the struggle of any director for his or her own distinctive style in tension with the accompanying pressures and compromises involved in raising money, getting one's films shown, and finding sympathetic collaborators who might help translate one's vision. Potter has collaborated with some key figures, each of whom has a distinctive artistic style. Rose English, Lindsay Cooper, and Jacky Lansley were performers in their own right before and after their involvement in Potter's cinema. Alexei Rodionov is a senior cinematographer, renowned in particular for *Idi I smotri* (Come and see; dir. Elim Klimov, 1985), and Hervé Schneid has edited the distinctive work of Jean-Pierre Jeunet (*Delicatessen,* 1991; and *Amélie,* 2001).

Potter's working practices, and her resulting films, represent an exploration of the problems encountered by women who seek a room of their own. Virginia Woolf's inquiry into the inequality of the sexes begins with the questioning hypothesis, "Women are poorer than men because . . . ?" (Woolf, *Room* 48), a question that is also pertinent to *Thriller*, with its analysis of the injustices done to a poor flower maker by a group of artists and the conventions of opera. The inequality between the sexes also forms the background to Potter's other films. We see it configured in cinematic terms as the male character's control over narrative; in social and legal terms, in the way *Orlando* as a woman loses her inheritance and is not supposed to appear in public alone; or in cultural and artistic terms, through the Argentinean tango, in which power depends on an agreement between partners. *The Tango Lesson* could be seen as the reinstatement of the creative process that was elided in *Orlando*. Also, in this film Potter adds further elements to Woolf's list of obstructions to women creating: the need to distance oneself from the world through time spent on one's own, writing a script, and the observational perspective that one must adopt in the world to be able to feed one's experiences into one's creative work. Potter's various onscreen observers become substitute "Sallys"—creators in their own right, given the task of watching the world go by and drawing from it.

The reflexivity of *The Tango Lesson*, its contemplation of what it means to be a woman filmmaker, makes it an invaluable text in this narrative of creativity. Several of Potter's early films make visible the transition from Sally Potter, the performance artist, singer, dancer, and choreographer who also dabbles in film, to Sally Potter, filmmaker and director. Most interestingly, the power that is involved in the simple act of stepping back from being a performer in front of the audience/camera to being a director behind the camera is apparent through a comparison of Potter's first film *Jerk*, featuring another avant-garde filmmaker, Mike Dunford, with one of Dunford's *Four Films* (1969), in which Potter is featured.

In the opening image of *Jerk*, a man (Dunford) faces us and is framed from the shoulders up. He has dark hair and a beard and looks straight into the camera, immediately piercing the fourth wall. Soon after we have registered this image, the face is made to move in unnatural ways through superimposition. Throughout this superimposition, backgrounds change, getting lighter and darker, and we register what look like male and female faces, with a medley of face shapes and hairstyles and differing light levels, from overexposed to very dark. The effect is such that the man now bobs about, flickering and shifting in appearance. His frontal position suggests a nonillusionist "performance" rather than an illusionist fiction. After about fifty seconds of this there is a cut, and the sequence ends with black leader—a reference to the materiality of film.

When light is restored to the screen, we see the same man's face, although this time it is out of focus. We are made aware of the camera lens as focus is restored. This time we stay with the face, shot against a white background. The face looks around, and there are jump cuts and then zooms as he tilts his head backwards and falls out of frame. Once again, he stares at us. He takes a photo—of us—then wipes sleep out of his eye, an act filmed in slow motion, extracting gesture from reality. Despite the fact that the frontal placement of this figure means that there was never a "fourth wall" illusionism, when he takes the photo it still seems to shatter a taboo. The thin line between camera and subject, director and actor, or looker and looked at is crossed as our object suggests that he might, in turn, be able to transform us into objects.

This moment is the climax of an exploration of shifts in power from subject to director that pervades the entire film. On the one hand, Potter seems to have control of her subject, since she has manipulated his image. On the other hand, although he allows himself to be framed, the man's stance, his look, and his actions are defiant, implying that he is in control. Three short sequences follow. In the first, the man is against a wall; in the second, he has changed his jacket, and he looks down, averting his gaze; in the third, the scene has changed entirely as we frame then zoom in to a window of a house. The ending of the film suggests that its mode might have been one of inquiry into the man as subject and the power of the camera to enter a space—as if peeping through a window.

Jerk serves as an example of a well-worn genre of filmmaking: the first films of future directors, which are used to define their early preoccupations, interests, and angle on cinema. The assumption frequently made is that, although personal style develops with practice, a kernel of personality will be present in a director's first few attempts at filmmaking. What is most apparent in *Jerk* is the experimental intentions of the images. Superimposition, zooming, and jump cuts are "tried out" for their effects on a standing subject. The relationship between camera and subject is tentatively explored, and Potter subjects the body to a variety of visual distortions. Nevertheless, the real power relationship is represented in "live" mode, as the man faces the camera and undertakes tasks that Potter may or may not have instructed. The moment in which he takes a photo of "us" is disarming, since he shifts from being the object of our gaze to being the subject who will not be objectified. Even at this early stage in her career, Potter reveals ambivalence about wielding the power of her camera.

Around the same time as *Jerk*, Potter "starred" in one part of Mike Dunford's *Four Films*. In *Four Films*, we find some of the same experimentation with equipment and subject as in *Jerk*. In the first three films, a combination of subjects completing actions (someone walks, someone puts foodstuff on their hair) and experiments with camera, focus, and editing makes for an interesting mix. In the fourth film, more happens. Dunford has described the film thus: "A girl walking across a piece of waste ground, an airplane flies over, a train goes past, and she walks away. It wasn't narrative but it was still a manipulation of events" (Dunford 87). The film opens with the Paramount logo, as if it were a blockbuster production, followed by a tilt down from the sky to a block of flats in the distance. A yard in the foreground reveals a woman walking towards us; the woman is Sally. She wears a long dark coat and has flowing red hair. She approaches the camera, which pans to the left away from her, revealing wasteland. This shot is cut as we hear an airplane overhead. We cut back to the woman, who is still walking, head down, hands in pockets, and she continues until out of frame. As she disappears, we cut quickly to a high-angled close-up of her face tilted up to the camera. She walks out of frame once more. We cut to a train and follow it, and the camera bobs around as if to mimic a walking motion. The opening sequence is repeated, but the footage is scratched and colored. As we cut to the close-up, there is a new cut to even closer on the face, followed by the Paramount logo.

Jerk and the fourth of *Four Films* share a similar intent: to frame a subject and see how that subject can be altered by editing, camera movement, and other effects. The differences between the two films are also notable. *Jerk* has Dunford frontally placed and staring at the camera. There is no attempt to create a diegetic, fictional space—what is created is a performance space. *Four Films*, by contrast, does begin with a "real" space into which its subject walks, thereby undertaking real actions. Into this situation the camera intrudes with its close-up on

Potter, who is still going about daily actions. Both subjects look at the camera, but whereas Potter's close-up comes about through an edit from Dunford, and is therefore still largely in his hands, in *Jerk,* with no edit, Dunford's look and then his action with the camera suggest a challenge to Potter's control. As a subject, Potter is replaying the conventional role of the vulnerable, passive woman. As a first-time director she is aware of—and resistant to—the power play that the leap to behind the camera implies. *Jerk* suggests that Potter's first forays into film were highly experimental, playing around with what she could do with the new medium; it also suggests that she is aware of her own position of power once behind the camera and enjoys exploring cinema's difference from the kind of critical and conceptual spaces she had been accustomed to with her own performance work.

Potter's ambivalent camera manifests itself in her features as a rejection of omnipotence. In *The Tango Lesson,* Pablo asks if Sally is looking at him; if so, what does she see when she does?

> Sally: I see you onscreen.
> Pablo: Then you're not here with me. You've become a camera.
> Sally: But that is how I love you . . . with my eyes.

This use of the camera—to love, to inquire, or to explore its subject—is based upon very different relationships of power and vulnerability, knowledge and complicity, subject and object, looker and looked at. Yet again these relationships have more to do with live performance than they do with the conventional subject-object relations we would identify with the cinema. One reason for this difference from conventions could be Potter's own experiences as a performer, through which she has been subjected to the gaze; therefore in her filmmaking she critiques this unbalanced situation. In the exhibition catalog for "About Time," a 1980 collection of mixed media, live art, and video, Lynn MacRitchie suggests that live and mixed media work "seems to suit women, to answer some of their creative needs. Many have confirmed in conversation that they are drawn to the area because of its lack of hierarchy and the opportunity for exploration it provides" (MacRitchie, *About Time* 29). Potter also writes in this catalog about women working in performance.

The distinctions she makes between acting and performance have some relevance to her own filmmaking:

> Performance is seen as "doing"—an activity which is being watched rather than a part being played. Characterization is seen as technique founded on a literary tradition heavily reliant on the written and spoken word and intimately connected with the aesthetics of illusionism which transport the spectator by a series of identificatory processes to another place and time by contrast; the performance artist is often concerned to alert the audience to the shifting constructions of the performance to be both inside and outside it, commenting on it. (Potter, "On Shows" 6)

Potter evidently is familiar with the perils of the gaze on the female body. All of her work on- and offscreen has addressed the vulnerability of the performer, the operations of existing standards of appearance and judgment, and the difficulties a director encounters in trying to escape the signification of the female body, given the dominant ways in which it has been seen. Of this she has said, "Woman as entertainer is a history of varying manifestations of female oppression, disguised, romanticized . . . the female performer has been visible; positioned always in relation to the male construction of femininity and in relation to male desire. Women performance artists, who use their bodies as the instrument of their work, constantly hover on the knife edge of the possibility of joining this spectacle of woman" (Potter, "On Shows" 6).

The highly performed actions and hesitant camera we find in *Jerk* signal the ways in which Potter would continue to place her actors in front of her camera. Ten years later, *Thriller* opens with Colette frontally placed and looking directly at the camera. This challenging gaze is followed by an examination of the recurring ways in which women have been looked at and judged, either for their appearance (Musetta), their economic status (Mimi), or their actions (Marion in *Psycho*). At the same time, *Thriller* refuses to allow these kinds of looks and judgments in its images; instead, it creates a visual world that combines the abstract and nonfictional with the staged and symbolic. At the time of its making, these directorial decisions were read positively by a feminist film practice that refused to use the seductive qualities of the female body in its films. Other examples include Chantal Akerman, who, in *Jeanne Dielman 23 quai du commerce 1080 Bruxelles* (1975), meticulously recorded the joyless existence of a Belgian housewife in a supreme act of antiseduction; or *Film about a Woman Who . . .* (1974) by Yvonne Rainer, which used a mixture of photographs, staged scenes, and intertitles to fragment its take on women and melodrama. Potter has spoken of feeling "human" rather than merely female and wanting to write from multiple points of view (Florence 284). The lack of objectifying shots and the use of editing to create looks at the female protagonist span Potter's works, as her male and female bodies are allowed to live in screen space without the camera subjecting them to a controlling gaze, scrutinizing them, or endlessly cutting them into close-up fragments.

So what *does* her camera do? And what replaces the patriarchal attitudes and linear singlemindedness of conventional cinema? Potter's personal style is inherent in her first two films and fully developed across the last four. The consistencies of camera work, editing, and a reverse-look figure all connect her films to her performance origins and suggest her authorial signature as a film director. Potter's camera is neither unobtrusive nor controlling. Several of her characters are observers who watch and comment on the unfolding events with looks or words. It is as if this frees her camera from an observational stance—it becomes a player as much as the characters. Generally, Potter's camera, directed by internationally acclaimed cinematographers, is impatient and reactive. It assertively arrives at scenes before characters rather than shyly following them. It rarely frames and then leaves alone; it is constantly moving with the characters to keep their figures in frame, or moving independent of them to suggest relationships between bodies and space. Similarly, her editing—by Hervé Schneid in *Orlando, The Tango Lesson,* and *The Man Who Cried* and Daniel Goddard in *YES*—is restrained yet expressive, allowing performances, music, dialogue, and movement to dictate its rhythm and frequency.

Several stylistic rules can be identified across Potter's last four features. First, spaces are rarely seen empty of people; instead we begin a scene after someone has entered a space, eliding the travel in between. This ellipsis of unimportant details is carried through to the endings of scenes, which do not always conclude by seeing people leave. The driving motion of Potter's narratives is propelled by swift edits as well as through point-of-view structures and the use of music and sound over edits. Shot–reverse-shot setups often miss off the final reverse shot that might reinforce a reaction we already know, and music from a subsequent scene frequently provides the cue for a cut, as if what happens next were waiting in the wings, impatiently, and pushing things along. Potter's style of rapid transitions from scene to scene, coupled with a rarely still camera, actively discourages the contemplation of the film's images. Perhaps for this reason the effect they have on us is immediate, and the strong intervention of a moving camera and brusque edits are designed to keep communicating. Finally, camera and editing are reinforced by the reverse look of characters that cements the bridge between audience and film.

In Potter's first featurette, *Thriller,* the first time we see Colette she is facing the camera and laughing. *Orlando* also has its main character look straight at us as he utters his first line, and *YES* begins with a cleaner candidly eying us as she whispers to camera. Film theory has claimed that these reverse looks shatter the illusion of reality that the fictional filmic experience traditionally tries to create. Classical cinema creates a sealed fictional space that retains the "fourth wall" and never directly addresses or acknowledges us. By contrast, the look back or reverse look gives us a storytelling style that is far more knowing and playful as it directly acknowledges that it is creating illusions. This kind of film practice has not typically been associated with fiction feature films but has been used by the avant-garde and counter-cinema. The aim of these experimental cinemas was to jolt the spectator from his or her forgetfulness and immersion in a story. The idea was to force the audience to stand back from films, aware of their complicity with capitalist, patriarchal ideology, to adopt a reflective attitude and active, intellectual engagement. *Thriller* takes part in this kind of deconstructive practice, as does *The Gold Diggers.*

However, in *Orlando* and the films that follow, these looks invite the audience in and suggest that we might share in this protagonist's commentary on the fictional world before us. The effect echoes what Wheeler Winston Dixon has called "the reciprocal gaze" (Dixon 3). Potter's reverse looks should be seen as chances not to stand apart from her films but to create bridges of reciprocation. The fact that all of her reverse-look protagonists are women is significant, since it gives these characters authority over the point of view of the story. Even though they may not have power in narrative terms, they can and will turn to us and comment, whereas other characters cannot and do not. Potter gives the reverse look to characters that have little authority in the stories themselves: Colette, who as Mimi is circumscribed by the story of *La Bohème;* Orlando, whose life will be governed by social gender conventions; and a cleaner and other cleaners, whose labor and unique position as viewers on the world go otherwise unseen.

Potter's reverse look creates a situation that is closer to her performance pieces than it is to conventional cinematic practice. From *Jerk* onwards, the overt inclusion of the audience through direct address is combined with a theatricalization that manifests itself through particular aspects of performance. These include the use of performers as well as actors, segmentation of a longer narrative into performed pieces, mini-performances within a larger drama, and an overemphasis on artifice and illusion that thereby foregrounds both.

The look back at us signals a particular attitude to illusionism, suggesting that Potter is more interested in the capacity to communicate to an audience on an equal footing than enticing us to forget our part in the unfolding of the narrative. The asides to camera given by Orlando actually invite us in, ask us to share, and label us as the only "company" that stays with him during his ill treatment of his fiancée, lack of talent as a poet, inability to fight "like a man," sex change, and loss of heritage. As Catherine Elwes notes when talking about live performance work, "Eye contact . . . told us that we were engaged in a social interaction and that the outcome of that encounter, the work itself, was unpredictable, risky, and in principle as much our responsibility as it was the artist's" (Elwes 196).

The story that is smacked on the publisher's desk in the final part, "Birth," could not have been written without us—indeed, it could be seen as the spectator's collaboration with Orlando that has brought this about. In this way, Potter adopts the role of creator only as long as it keeps her in contact with her audience. Through her observer-characters, her conscious camera, and brusque editing, the creation that is taking place remains evident. Ironically, then, and as we will see in her films to follow, Potter's "frame of her own" becomes a window that she opens to invite us in rather than a screen that we are expected to see through.

Absent Women and Tales Taken Apart:
Thriller and *The Gold Diggers*

Thriller

At thirty-five minutes, *Thriller* is slightly too long for a short and not quite developed enough for a feature. This awkward length also reflects the experimental nature of the film, which repeats some of the preoccupations with how bodies in space are affected by editing and framing in Potter's early films. *Thriller* also explores the place of the heroine within the genres of operatic melodrama and the cinematic thriller.

At the time of its release, *Thriller* was widely praised as a feminist classic. For E. Ann Kaplan, the film "attempts . . . to link psychoanalytic, feminist, and Marxist discourses" (Kaplan, "Night" 115), and for B. Ruby Rich, it "goes farther than many feminist films. It not only reclaims the past, not only re-reads the official history in terms of the present, but also dares to imagine the future" (Rich, "Prologue" 228). The premise of all feminist interventions in the cinema has been that the position of women is unequal: men have controlled filmmaking and therefore image making, as well as film history and thus the interpretation of those images. Therefore, the first objective of all feminist attention has been to reveal the female. This was not an easy task, given the consensus that the feminine had been largely absent from film and the worry that any attempt to identify it might lead to essentialism. For Teresa De Lauretis, the term "woman" refers to "a fictional construct" (5), and for Claire Johnston, "woman is presented as what she represents for man" (25).

Thriller is essentially a feminist retelling of Giacomo Puccini's opera *La Bohème* (first performed in Turin in 1896). However, its structure is not straightforward, a fact reflected in the way that reviews all feel the need to summarize it in detail. Critics typically make their case for *Thriller* as a film that either merely takes apart found narratives or that also offers something new. Kaplan, for example, notes that Potter ambitiously attempts to link "psychoanalytic, feminist, and Marxist discourses" ("Night" 115) and thereby bring together key concerns of feminist film theory, as found in the work of Laura Mulvey and Claire Johnston. For Kaplan, Potter's film "offers the possibility for change" and a "suggestion of hope" ("Night" 122) through its deconstruction of the doomed love story and classic thriller. The sense that the film suggests a way forward without enacting it is echoed by Joan Copjec, who explores *Thriller* from a psychoanalytic perspective. For Copjec, Mimi's decipherment of her murder is comparable to the oedipal patricide narrative, and *Thriller* becomes interesting as a film about identification and the formation of subjectivity. Jane Weinstock constructs her own lyrical questioning process around the film's opening image of the laughing Colette, and Julia Kristeva's work is key to her interpretation. For Weinstock, *Thriller* becomes as much about evoking semiotics ("that which summons the pre-rational, that time before the subject, before the object, the point of no return" [103]) as psychoanalysis.

For many critics, *Thriller* shows how certain narratives and discourses hide their patriarchal agenda. However, for B. Ruby Rich and Annette Kuhn, the film goes further than this by offering a vision of "reconstruction." Kuhn discusses *Thriller* alongside *Lives of Performers* (dir. Yvonne Rainer, 1972), *Daughter Rite* (dir. Michelle Citron, 1978), and *Jeanne Dielman 23 Quai du Commerce 1080 Bruxelles* (dir. Chantal Akerman, 1975) as films that write the feminine into the visual and narrative structures of cinema (Kuhn 164). She suggests that such films offer examples of the pleasures of experiencing female stories, watching female characters, and experiencing a female gaze (that of the character or director). For Kuhn, *Thriller* is part of a feminist counter-cinema; in this same spirit, Rich names the film as a prime example of "oppositional" or "reconstructive" practice ("In the Name" 281)—her other example is *Daughter Rite*. According to Rich, *Thriller* distinguishes itself by its "rebuilding of other forms . . . according to feminist specifications . . . reconstructing forms in a constructive manner" (281–82).

These examples of how *Thriller* was seen by critics and theorists at the time of its release indicate perceptions of its importance as a practical illustration and working through of theoretical problems (women's place as other in narrative, the problematic construction of female subjectivity) and its enunciation of wider social issues (women's unequal place in a capitalist, patriarchal society). This dual appeal to film theory and the wider world continues in *The Gold Diggers* and *Orlando*, where the blame for the suppression of the main characters is explored in terms of narrative as well as cultural and social structures.

My analysis of *Thriller* will begin with the issue of retelling. The film introduces us to Colette Laffont, who will act as the investigator who takes us through the opera, trying to reread it as the story of Mimi. The story of the opera is told: In 1830, in the Latin Quarter of Paris, Mimi lives in an attic above four artists, Rodolfo, a poet; Schaunard, a musician; Marcello, a painter; and Colline, a philosopher. Mimi is a seamstress who works as many hours as she can making silk flowers to sell at the market.

We are also introduced to Musetta, a "loose woman" who was once the lover of Marcello. On the way upstairs one evening, Mimi's candle is blown out, forcing her to knock on the door below. She meets Rodolfo, and they fall in love. Rodolfo later learns that she is ill; unable to bear her suffering, he breaks off their relationship. Mimi gets increasingly ill, until one evening Musetta takes her to the artists and says that she is dying. Mimi dies lying on a bed while Rodolfo weeps.

Colette returns to this story again and again, rereading details from Mimi's point of view. Throughout this rereading—and also prompting it—we see performers in Colette's attic who act out some of her conclusions. We also see still images that seem to be reconstructions of a crime scene and hear the famous shower-scene music from Alfred Hitchcock's *Psycho,* thus widening the scope of the notion of women whom narrative has abused. *Thriller* ends with Colette/Mimi's realization that the tragedy was at her expense—that she was actually absent as a subject, had to die young, and as a consequence never got to know Musetta.

The experimental attitude we find in Potter's short films is extended in *Thriller,* which uses complex combinations of media such as stills from "live" action and images from recorded performance to suggest the telling and retelling. Dance and choreographed movement play an equally important part alongside voiceover, dialogue, and the physical interaction of the performers. The body signifies on different levels: Colette Laffont could be Colette the narrator, or Mimi, or simply a dancer. The repetition of the still photographs suggests the action of the story (for example, Musetta is seen entering the room) and the frozen symbolism of a moment that is otherwise outside of the narrative (Mimi and Musetta "could have been friends"). As with *Jerk,* Potter's personal style—her control over her camera, editing, and mise-en-scène—were still developing. However, the collage effect she creates by showing one narrative, such as Colette asking questions, while referring to another narrative through opera music on the sound track layers sound and image in a way that we will also find in *The Gold Diggers*. Key concerns of Potter's can be identified, such as women being able to tell their own stories and the significance of the performing body as a language system equal to voiceover.

Thriller commences with black leader. Like many feminist films from this time (such as Lis Rhodes's *Light Reading* [1978]), this "blank" suggests that we not take images for granted; instead, what we *are* shown is significant. The blank screen also suggests that we must adjust our prejudices, which force a hierarchy between looking and listening in the cinema, and listen attentively. (In Potter's later film, *YES*, although the visual is important and is treated as such, thematically and formally we are asked to listen—to the voices of others, to the resonances and hidden meanings of the verse—more intently than we might otherwise.)

After a few seconds of blackness at the start of *Thriller*, we hear the moment from the end of *La Bohème* when Rodolfo discovers that Mimi is dead and sings "Mimi, Mimi!" In the film, the opera is never "acted out" visually; we only hear this recording and see representative still photos from it. What we hear is the outpouring of grief through Rodolfo's cry. This is effectively the most emotional scene in the opera, and Potter immediately gives away its ending. Mimi is already dead, the demands of operatic convention have determined her fate, and Rodolfo's grief has supplanted Mimi's suffering. Colette must begin at the end and use repetition, deconstruction, and collage to reread this ending.

Thriller then fades up to reveal Colette on a chair in the corner of a bare attic room. There is immediately a strangeness about the mixing of the authentic setting—an attic—with Colette's modern and thus "inauthentic" appearance. This is our first clue that what follows will not be acting in the typical sense but something closer to performance art. Colette slams a book shut and begins to laugh. Her laugh has been widely discussed, and despite the different critical readings of *Thriller*, all reviews agree on the importance of the sound track. For Kuhn, the woman's voice is "privileged" and becomes one way of foregrounding the otherwise repressed "feminine" (163). For Copjec, Weinstock, and Rich, Colette's voiceover and her laugh, the scream from *Psycho*, and the operatic sound track all suggest that we take notice of sound as equally expressive as the image.

We are invited to compare Rodolfo's cry and Colette's laugh: both are nonverbal expressions of emotion that suggest that the film's retelling of *La Bohème* will be at the expense of the men. Colette's laugh also provides us with our second ending. As her constant questioning finishes with her searching for a theory that would explain her/Mimi's life, she asks, "Was the clue to my death written in their text?" She turns to these books, reads aloud, then laughs, and answers, "No wait, the clue." We return to the opera with a dissolve to a photograph of a stage set of an attic, also accompanied by opera music. The attic/stage of this photo and the attic with Colette in it are juxtaposed. The framing of fiction within fiction is completed by the sudden sound of the distinctive music from *Psycho*'s shower scene.

In the opening minutes of *Thriller*, sound and image—and sometimes sound or image—conjure up three different spaces, stories, and performers such that the viewer must work pretty hard. The first story space is that of the opera, although this is only ever "seen" as the account given by Colette/Mimi and the production stills. The second is Colette's space, which is given no definite historical time or geographical place but seems to be simply the black box of performance, where she acts out Mimi's story as she retells it. We might also compare this space to the inside of the hut in *The Gold Diggers*, where Celeste takes Ruby, or to the creative space we share with Orlando in the opening of that film, as he sits with quill poised. We can also compare the bare room of *The Tango Lesson*, with its blank table/canvas, to the attic in *Thriller*: in both, Potter is trying to rewrite a story. This space can be seen as a creative "room of one's own": Mimi is doing work (though in other circumstances this would be considered "craft" or "skill"), and Sally is writing a film. Colette and Sally are both sitting, imagining other worlds, as if the room is a cinema in which reveries come to life.

This comparison between Colette and Sally reminds us that all of Potter's films feature figures who cross time and space. It's not that her characters are homeless; they simply like to travel and to experience, and new places seem to indicate new challenges to their identity. In *Thriller*, Colette, a French woman, performs in a British director's film about a Parisian seamstress set in a London attic. In *The Gold Diggers*, Colette again inhabits a city that combines clichéd elements with specific spaces, and some action takes place in Iceland.

In *Thriller*, we encounter this attic as a "live" space with real, moving bodies before it is transformed by the still photos of Colette that are shown over the *Psycho* music. This music brings us to our third space, a remembered thriller that has clear parallels with *La Bohème*. Mimi in the opera and Janet Leigh's character in the film (Marion) serve the narrative purpose of acting as our introduction to the male characters Rodolpho and Norman Bates, respectively. Despite Marion's active role in stealing the money so that she and her married lover can be together, her story goes nowhere, since the film is not about her. Although she sets things in motion, the baton of the plot will be passed to Norman, and then we have to wait before the discovery of the end of Marion's story. Similarly, although *La Bohème* is known as a tragic love story, only rarely do we hear of Mimi's position; instead, Rodolpho gives us his point of view. The many photos that recur in *Thriller* are like the screens that played behind Potter's dancers in her early expanded-cinema work. They problematize the presentness and presence of Colette in the attic. They circulate in a space between storytelling and story told. Like the two endings with which we begin, they suggest the circularity of the film, which undermines the linear shape upon which *La Bohème* relies for its tragedy. The multimedia nature of the opening also suggests that Potter has not really chosen cinema over dance, photography, opera, or music; she will use all of these to create her collage of meaning on screen.

Colette Laffont functions as an interrogator who takes the narrative of *La Bohème* apart. She also critiques the ritual sacrifice of women in the name of tragedy, the romanticization of poverty, and the creation of feminine stereotypes by ballet, opera, cinema, and economic inequality. Laffont herself represents a challenge to our expectations, as a black woman with a French accent whose racial identity does not define her. Neither is she defined by gender, since she looks androgynous and plays the roles of Mimi/victim and Mimi/investigator. In a sense, Colette can be read as a precedent to Orlando: someone without sex or gender connotations to whom we are persuaded to relate. The same might be said of the cleaner in *YES*, who, in her white cleaning coat and hygienically tied back hair, comes across as a similarly desexualized character.

Colette's quest, prompted by her opening questions—"Did I die? Was I murdered? If so, who killed me and why? What does it mean?"—has echoes of Woolf's opening question in *A Room of One's Own:* "Women are poorer than men because?" (48). *Thriller* undertakes a comparable exploration of the inaccessibility of certain spaces to women and the roles that they have been assigned. Woolf's comment—"Women have served all these centuries as looking-glasses possessing the magic and delicious power of reflecting the figure of man at twice its natural size" (53)—is echoed in Colette's findings: "I had to be young, single, and vulnerable to serve their desire to become heroes in the display of their grief." There is another echo of Woolf's astonishment at the rarity with which novels by women depict women as friends rather than rivals:

> "Chloe liked Olivia," I read. And then it struck me how immense a change was there. Chloe liked Olivia perhaps for the first time in literature. Cleopatra did not like Octavia . . . how interesting it would have been if the relationship between the two women had been more complicated. All these relationships between women, I thought . . . are too simple. So much has been left out, unattempted. (123)

In *Thriller*, Colette/Mimi's narration tells us: "If Musetta had died it would not have been a tragedy, for she was an easy woman, a bad girl . . . we were set up as opposites and complementary characters and kept apart to serve our roles. Yes, it was murder. We never got to know each other. Perhaps we would have loved each other."

The route Potter travels from Colette's opening question to her bitter conclusions involves a variety of devices. First, there is the verbal telling and retelling of the story of *La Bohème*, three times. What begins as a straight retelling ("I am told the story is this . . ."), where Colette delivers the official, romantic version as we might find it in a theater program, shifts to a lingering on details ("I am trying to understand . . ."), where Mimi is able to see from an omniscient position. She now knows that Rudolpho hid her key. This concludes with her analysis of every part of the story, seeking clues and answers: "No, wait . . . the clue. Suddenly I understand." She alleges a conspiracy to "produce the story to disguise how I must produce their goods" and to have her die so that she remains young and childless, the defining traits of the romantic heroine.

The shifts that Colette/Mimi undergoes enable her to take apart the narrative and see the bourgeois, romantic assumptions on which it rests, and they seem dependent on a different point of view. This theme recurs across Potter's films. *Orlando's* "same person, different sex" implies that the way of seeing and being does not change, and the cleaner's closing words in *YES*—"When you look closer, nothing goes away, / It changes, see, like night becomes a day, / And day the night. . . . / It's really all about your point of view"—firmly reiterate *Thriller*'s starting point. As Mimi, Colette could see only her own part in the story, but in the second retelling she is better able to read the actions of the men and blame them for her demise. The shift in point of view is initially brought about through the mirror into which Colette keeps looking for clues. E. Ann Kaplan has suggested that Mimi has to go back to the mirror phase: "[S]he needs to understand how her subjectivity was constituted and deal with herself as split subject in a symbolic order dominated by the Father" (Kaplan, "Night" 116). This reading assumes that Mimi is seeking to find or express her "real" identity, and as we have seen, there is such a strong use of acting out, standing in for, and doubling when it comes to the rules for reading from person to body that any sense of Colette "really" being Mimi or English "really" being Musetta is dispelled. Instead, the mirror should be seen as a screen that situates Colette as both actor/Mimi and spectator/Mimi.

This reading is apparent from the opening sequence, which finishes with Colette facing us with her hand over her mouth. She has her back to the mirror, yet we see not the reflection of her back but the duplicate image of her, face forward and hand over mouth.

This is the first of a series of distortions of the "double" that mean that identity is confused across the film. The mirror does not show us the "reality" of Colette—what cannot be seen from the front. Instead, it gives us a repeated image of what we already can see. The mirror therefore becomes an instrument not of reflection but of reflexivity—a surface that has no depth but refers to itself (and the rest of the film) self-consciously. The first time this happens, a doubling of Mimi occurs that allows her to be in the story and stand outside and comment on it. In the mirror sequence with Musetta, Colette's recognition of herself as other concludes with, "And then as her image turned away I saw the other side. Was it me?" The splitting commences as Colette begins her second telling of the story, saying, "*I* was going up the stairs" instead of "She."

The second path taken to get from beginning to end involves the other performers, captured in still photographs and moving images. The function of these performers shifts. At times they "act out" according to

Mimi (Colette Laffont) in *Thriller* retells the story
of *La Bohème* three times. Photo by Sally Potter.
© Adventure Pictures Ltd.

Colette/Mimi's recollection; thus, as Colette says, "Oh Mimi, you were
carried out of the room . . . in arabesque, in arabesque yes I was," we
see a close-up of a woman (English) with her leg held in arabesque by
a man. This cuts to a wider shot in which we see that she is actually
held by two men.

English stands in for Mimi and Musetta at different times. The
opening arabesque shots are followed by Colette's first telling of the *La
Bohème* story. Colette sits in front of the mirror and says, "When she
first looked," and we cut to an extreme close-up of Colette's face. The
line that follows—"She recognized herself as the other"—is accompanied by the same shot of English/Musetta's face. We cut back to Mimi
and see English in the background. The two men perform as partners
to the dancing women, supporting English in arabesque, for example,
and also stand in for the main men in the opera, Rodolfo and Marcello,
as they sit on the chair and are interrogated by the camera under noir-
esque lighting, or pretend to box with Colette as she asks, "Was there a

Musetta (Rose English) performs the classically
feminine arabesque. Photo by Sally Potter.
© Adventure Pictures Ltd.

fight?" Their final act, climbing out of the window as Mimi and Musetta embrace, suggests that they were Colette's pawns, condemned to act in her drama as she wished.

Like Potter's early mixed-media performances, in which "live" dancers moved in front of recorded moving images, *Thriller*'s juxtaposition of moving footage and still photos creates a kind of Chinese-box effect: we are not sure which is the moment of telling, which images are in the past and which the present. Thus the opening image of Colette laughing on the chair might seem to be the "now" of the film, yet it is repeated later and revealed to be a part of the investigation that happened in the past. Effectively, this makes the initial laughter sequence a flashback. However, the conventional rules of narrative logic, time, and space cannot be applied to *Thriller.* The only "now" of the film—the only action that has not occurred before the film starts—is Colette's investigation and conclusions. It is Colette who gathers visual evidence from past and present occurrences and mixes them up to settle her quest. Although she has reached a point of conclusion, having answered the question of whether she was murdered or not, there is no space in this film to explore the subjunctive world she offers at the end: "Perhaps we [Mimi and Musetta] would have loved each other."

Since the men have exited out the window, the embrace of Musetta/English and Mimi/Laffont suggests the creation of a women-only space open to friendships and relationships between women. The possibility of a sexual relationship developing between Mimi and Musetta is posed by the voiceover. In the context of the opera, such a relationship would, of course, have been highly subversive. However, the filmmaking context from which *Thriller* emerged, which was part of a countercultural discourse strongly influenced by feminist, black, and gay and lesbian politics, makes a lesbian relationship possible. The casting, costume, and choreography support this possibility. Colette Laffont is an androgynous-looking performer, whose short hair and loose trouser suit could support a reading of her as "butch." By contrast, Rose English has a stereotypically feminine or "femme" appearance, with long hair that often hangs around her face and a knee-length skirt. Further, English "dances" the female role, with her arabesque and her lifts provided by the two men. Laffont's movements are unconventional: as the two men lift her and turn her upside down, she boxes with them and asks, "Would I ever be the hero?" This question is followed by a scene in which one man wears a tutu over his trousers, and she lifts him up. The subversive possibilities of Laffont mixing up our understanding of feminine and masculine behavior and taking on the male role in narrative and performance are developed further in *The Gold Diggers*, before also feeding into *Orlando*. The "queer" sensibility of *Orlando* was the delight of many critics and audiences (see Barrett; Cummins; and Hankins), but the film's heterosexualization of Woolf's main character was also criticized by those eager to see how Potter would adapt Woolf's supposed love letter to the lesbian Vita Sackville-West.

To return to the final scene of *Thriller*, although this space seems to be exclusive of men, with Potter's later films in mind we can read it instead as a space aside from the patriarchal. In this nonpatriarchal space, women are not defined only as the other or the mirror to men; instead, they are free to look, tell, desire, and create. Significantly for *Thriller*, this is a performance space that is apart from the real world.

The challenge for Potter's film practice would be to take this space that she has struggled for in *Thriller* out in to the world and to reintroduce men without allowing patriarchy to destroy it.

The Gold Diggers

Potter's intention to exit the performance space of *Thriller* is reflected in the title of her next film, which refers to Busby Berkeley's musical *The Gold Diggers of 1933*. The oppositional attitude that Potter's film takes to Berkeley's film and backstage musicals in general is evident once we compare the openings of both films. Berkeley's film opens with his trademark parade of hundreds of women. Ginger Rogers, naked except for a large gold coin around her hips, a gold bra, and cloak, sings "We're in the Money," and the camera focuses on women with large gold coins draped around various parts of their bodies. The performance is watched by Barney Hopkin, a man with a fat cigar. The film then follows the efforts of three of these showgirls to find husbands. Polly (Ruby Keeler) forms a relationship with Brad (Dick Powell), a struggling songwriter who turns out to be the son of a millionaire. Brad's brother is sent—along with his advisor, Felonius—to bring him home and buy off the girl, but instead he is duped by Polly's roommates, Carol and Trixie. Despite telling them that in his opinion showgirls are "parasites, chisellers, and gold diggers," the brother falls for Carol, and Felonius falls for Trixie.

In Potter's film, the gold diggers are not the women using their wiles and charm to lure the men but men digging for gold in an icy, bare landscape. The value is reversed in Potter's film: the women become associated with gold, and, as Potter has indicated in her director's statement, their names—Celeste and Ruby—are meant to indicate that "their story evokes the alchemists' search for the 'celestial ruby' (the formula for creating gold)" (Potter, "Gold Diggers" 142).

This reference to alchemy should not be taken lightly, since the alchemists' elemental obsession is revisited across Potter's films in scenes that include water at moments of transformation. Specifically, we can cite the sex change of Orlando, when she washes her face. This is echoed by Suzy in *The Man Who Cried* and SHE in *YES*. By contrast, in *The Tango Lesson* it is Sally who washes Pablo's face. In all cases the moment at which these faces are washed suggests new beginnings for their characters, perhaps the prolongation of life, which was one of the goals of the alchemists. For Ruby (Julie Christie), the archetypal introspective feminine heroine, her value is measured in gold, while Celeste (Colette Laffont), associated with the more masculine, active investigation, uncovers "the secrets and rituals of ownership that lie behind the movement of money" (Potter, "Gold Diggers" 142).

In a 1993 interview with David Ehrenstein, Potter admitted, "After *The Gold Diggers* I was cinematically in the wilderness for a decade" (Ehrenstein, "Out of the Wilderness" 3), and within Potter's oeuvre, *The Gold Diggers* has been seen as the thorn in her side. The film attempts to explore many of the issues opened up by *Thriller* in a feature-length format. It was made in a national context in which directors who had worked within avant-garde models were looking to expand their ideas and engage with narrative's pleasures. Derek Jarman, Laura Mulvey, Peter Wollen, Isaac Julien, and Peter Greenaway are only a few of those who took up this challenge.

Greenaway and Potter were both supported by the British Film Institute (BFI) production board, which invited Potter to make a feature film on the back of her first short. The work of Potter, Greenaway, and later Jarman that the production board supported represents a renewal of the experimental impulse that had once characterized its output. British cinema during the early 1980s, the first few years of Margaret Thatcher's reign, was in flux. While the mainstream was dominated by heritage productions such as *Chariots of Fire* (dir. Hugh Hudson, 1981), this was also the moment of Hanif Kureshi and Stephen Frears's *My Beautiful Laundrette* (1985). In such a context, there was no "norm" against which to measure *The Gold Diggers*, which perhaps explains some of the critical indifference to the film.

The Gold Diggers is one of the few features for which Potter did not have to spend years raising money. However, she has had to struggle for it critically, justifying her commitment to theory, her resistance of closure, and her collage of sound, music, and image, narrative, dream, and metaphor. As with many misunderstood films, part of *The Gold Diggers'* mythic failure stems from its restricted exhibition. The film has not been available for viewing since its initial release, and even its broadcast on Channel Four in the U.K. produced a very poor copy. The copies that still exist do not reveal a "visually stunning" film (Rosenbaum 127) that showcases the talent for detailed and unusual composition that we later find in *Orlando*.

In the opening scene, the complexity and elegance of Potter's raw ideas are amply expressed. As antlike gold miners wind their way across an iconic empty space into the distance, on the sound track we hear repetitive piano music and a riddle. Images compete with sound, demanding that we look yet also giving us a thinking space. The juxtaposition of the narrative with the metaphoric is established. Few critics appreciated the division of attention that this film demands. For Jonathon Rosenbaum, who saw the film before it was officially released, it was "witty and pleasurably inventive throughout" (127). However, many critics failed to comprehend *The Gold Diggers*. Some years later, in 1988, Janet Maslin suggested that the film had had its day: "[T]his thing—a 1983 oddity, sort of a feminist, deconstructionist, riddle-filled anti-musical, much of it set on the Icelandic tundra—is pure torture. Its only noteworthy attribute is the presence of Julie Christie" (Maslin, "Julie" 18). On one level, Maslin is right. *The Gold Diggers* is indeed a "feminist, deconstructionist, riddle-filled anti-musical," yet the fact that she uses these terms to suggest its obsolesence reflects the negative connotations the term "feminist" had accrued by the end of the 1980s. Maslin is also correct in surmising that *The Gold Diggers* works best as an early 1980s experience. The film is best read against the background of an attack on the place of the woman in the visual pleasure matrix and a tentative response to the call for a counter-cinema to replace this dominant model.

This is not to suggest that the film's only value is in its ideas. Such a misguided reading typified the film's reception, with one critic suggesting, "[O]ne cannot help wondering whether, at the end of the day, an article would have expressed the filmmaker's idea in an easier—and more precise—way" (Hibbin 15). Hibbin misses the point; Potter has always been interested in cinema for its audio-visual attack, its power to affect a number of our senses at once. Despite her accomplishment as a writer of lyrics, performance pieces, and screenplays, and the fact that she could easily have written "an article," words alone would not have fully conveyed Potter's ideas. Potter has noted in interviews that in *The Gold Diggers* she was "pulling all the codes of cinema apart" (Indiana 88), and in a further attempt to explain its largely poor reviews, we might suggest that Potter's achievement was to give equal attention to her dialogue, sound track, and images. Although this creates a visually beautiful, aurally stimulating, and verbally witty experience, the three-pronged attack confounds viewers who are used to image dominating over sound or dialogue "clarifying" the visuals. *The Gold Diggers* confronts the inadequacies of our senses, overwhelming them and demanding our complete attention.

More than twenty years after it was made, the film does seem to represent a particular moment in feminist film history. Its deconstructive intent provides an experience that is witty, thought-provoking, and frequently surprising. Despite the borrowing of an investigator from film noir and the archetypal heroine, recognizable elements that lead to an investigation and a rescue, *The Gold Diggers* is also highly original. Its originality, along with its ambitious nature, could also help explain its poor critical reception. Although some critics praised it and engaged its complexities, most seem merely bewildered. Potter herself has lamented, "*Gold Diggers* was the greatest baptism by fire and the greatest learning experience of my life. . . . But I think the film was a monumental failure" (MacDonald, "Interview" 204). Nevertheless, in terms of Potter's development as a director, it is hard to imagine her making *Orlando* directly (albeit with the long gap) after *Thriller. The Gold Diggers* is a crucial film within her oeuvre since it develops cursory themes from *Thriller* and anticipates the union of Mimi and Musetta that recurs in *The Man Who Cried.* It also features haunting combinations of sound and image that make full use of the capacity of thirty-five-millimeter film for detail.

As with many of Potter's films, the opening weaves together several musical themes that recur throughout the film. First, we hear the song "Seeing Red," followed by a wilder-sounding track associated with the cold, icy landscape with which the film opens. Finally, we hear the repetitive music that accompanies the riddle "I am born in a beam of light." Like the collage effect achieved by *Thriller,* this opening sets up several layers and fictional worlds among which we flit for the rest of the film. These different layers also seem to offer different identifications. First, the song (sung by Potter) suggests a dissatisfied female spectator who has looked to film for something—"Went to the pictures for a break, / Thought I'd put my feet up, have a bit of intake"—that she clearly has not found: "But then, a man with a gun came in through the door, / And when he killed her, I couldn't take it anymore." Like the opening of *Thriller,* in which the received version of *La Bohème* is delivered, this song sets up the classical role of women and shows how inadequately it fulfills the needs of the female spectator. The consequence is clearly spelt out in the chorus of the song: "Please, please, please give me back my pleasure, / Please give me back my good night out, / Please give me back my leisure time, / I've got the pleasure-time blues, I'm seeing red."

One reading of this song might be that Potter is opening the way for what she intends to provide: pleasure for the female spectator that does not involve the death of the woman (à la *Psycho*) or her submission to the will of the hero or the demands of the narrative. She asserted around the time of the film's release, "Ultimately, my own desire was, and is, to give pleasure; to heal the 'pleasure-time blues' of the opening song" (Cook, "British" 13). However, the way in which she describes what her female spectator seeks—"a good night out" as part of her "leisure time and a rest"—do not exactly fit what *The Gold Diggers* delivers. The terms of spectatorship one might associate with switching off and taking time out are those against which most alternative work at this time rallied. The dialectic opened up at the beginning of *The Gold Diggers*—between the kind of cinema described in the song and that supplied by the film— suggests that Potter does not entirely deliver on her intentions.

This awkward beginning also reflects the fact that the film was made at a moment of transition in feminist film theory. *Thriller* represents a practical exploration of Laura Mulvey's influential essay "Visual Pleasure and Narrative Cinema" (1975) in its lament that the role of woman in narrative is circumscribed by patriarchal demands. The film agrees with Mulvey that the future for the female is bleak, that she exists as one part of a binary opposition (male/female, active/passive, looker/ looked at), and that she therefore can do little to change the course of the narrative. For many feminist theorists who followed Mulvey, the bleakness of her message was amplified by the fact that she could not find an adequate (or pleasurable) place for the female spectator, who was condemned to identify with the male hero and thereby objectify the woman or, as she suggested in a later essay, identify masochistically with the female ("Afterthoughts").

Potter's lyrics to "Seeing Red" echo the ideas of many feminist critics in deploring the lack of active, desiring, and likeable women with whom women viewers could identify. These were not to be found in this first stage of feminist filmmaking—or films by women filmmakers—which was largely deconstructive, forbade illusionism and the suspension of disbelief, and strove to break up narratives in order to prevent the hegemonic imposition on the woman that took place once the narrative was in full flow. *The Gold Diggers* was made in the transitional period between the advocacy of a kind of anticinema—antinarrative, anti-illusionist, and by extension antipleasure—and the movement towards feminist interventions in the mainstream. By the late 1970s and early 1980s, conditions were changing so that low-budget filmmaking was no longer materially, aesthetically, politically, and theoretically viable (there was less money around and fewer chances to exhibit and distribute such films). This shift can partly be explained by changes in taste, as new fashions and trends took over. The rejection of the small-scale and unprofessional could be seen as a natural progression. After years of short or low-budget films, there was a call for feature films that aimed for bigger and better things from women directors. In short, what was demanded was "going mainstream," as noted by Michelle Citron: "Feminist film-makers had little desire to enter into the mainstream film world. We wanted to make films that challenged the status quo. . . . But in a changing political context, the dominant film world became more enticing" (45).

These shifts and contestations might further explain the poor reception of *The Gold Diggers,* which may have been perceived as reflecting an obsolete form of feminist film theory. However, it does offer us a "spectator" figure in the film with whom we might identify. Playing once again the role of observer and narrator, Colette/Celeste occupies such a position; if we follow this line of thought, she acts out several possible positions that a female spectator might adopt and from which she might gain several different sorts of pleasure. Following Potter's opening song, we are given the riddle, spoken presumably by Ruby, that sets her up as a figure of fascination for Celeste. The riddle expresses the paradox at the heart of cinema: it creates an illusion that does not really exist, but due to the conditions of the cinematic apparatus, we "believe" it (suspending our disbelief) for the length of the film. We hear:

I am born in a beam of light.
I move continuously, yet I am still.

I am larger than life yet do not breathe.
Only in the darkness am I visible.
You can see me yet never touch me.
I can speak to you yet never hear you.
You know me intimately, and I know you not at all.
We are strangers, yet you take me inside of you.
What am I?

Celeste follows this with: "Time is short. We have ninety minutes to find each other, to solve this riddle."

The kind of relationship suggested in the riddle is as bleak as that forecast by Colette for Mimi and Musetta. It is free from any real engagement or emotional ties. It is one of objectification and distance, of false intimacy and no real bond. Having presented this possibility for the "connection" between Celeste and Ruby, the film then offers other ways of thinking about how they might connect primarily through Celeste, who is a disruptive figure. Celeste's first role is as a surrogate hero: she will rescue Ruby from a dull series of suitors who pass her from one to another as if she were a package of little value, despite the grandness of her entrance into the ballroom. Celeste adopts the role of the male hero, taking charge, initiating Ruby's required search, and removing her from the gazes of other men. Colette/Celeste has her familiar androgynous appearance: short hair and tomboyish figure and trousers and top. From a shot of all the women who have run to the exit to follow the horse and riders (while all the men mill around at the back of the room, confused), we cut to a mythic shot in which the horse and riders gallop into the distance of a wide and empty landscape.

Celeste takes Ruby to the hut, an unidentified, sparsely furnished location with a spotlight and stagelike space and a chair that resembles the chair in the attic performance space in *Thriller*. Celeste paces around boldly, while Ruby sits with her skirts wide about her. Celeste treats Ruby like a subject under investigation, instructing, "Tell me everything you know." This demand leads to Ruby's remembrance of her mother with whom she was "always stranded." It appears that this is not the answer Celeste was hoping for, as she swiftly exits.

The sequence in which Celeste questions what she is doing seems designed to suggest an equivalence between the woman and gold and to effect a Lewis Carroll–like confusion of logic. This sequence also suggests some of the ways in which Celeste is not in control and emphasizes the patriarchal power that governs language and how it is used. Initially, Celeste begins by asking the man who paces her office, "Sir, I'd like to have some more information about these figures I'm typing." If Mimi questions her place in the economy in terms of how much it is preordained because of the norms of a class-driven society, then Celeste's intervention threatens those in charge, who rebuff her question with a refusal to explain or clarify. Instead they confuse, speak in riddles, and generally obstruct her at every turn. The answer to Celeste's first question is, "Just do your job"; in other words, "Don't ask questions or think." The next scene shows Celeste waiting. She is met by a series of bureaucratic maneuvers: she is asked if she has an appointment, told to sit in a different chair, and then asked the same questions again. It is only when she says she wants "information" that she is taken to the next stage in the game. This scene would seem to play out the fact that language is manmade and therefore needs to be used creatively by women.

Having asked for information, Celeste is led into a high-ceilinged room with a checkered floor (a further allusion to *Through the Looking Glass* and its game of chess). A man sits at an extremely high desk; Celeste must look up to make him out. As she explains what she wants to know, he repeats several words: "money, movement, specific, general," abstracting them from their sense. The man who had led her into the room begins to repeat the words of the second man, as if they are Wonderland's Tweedle-Dum and Tweedle-Dee. The scene ends with both men sitting on the floor with an upturned bench over their legs, as if the giant desk had suddenly shrunk. Once dwarfed by the furniture, it is as if they are now giants.

While this scene seems to defy logic, it also creates important links between the woman and gold. At one point, the first man—who moves around various pieces of furniture—brings two columns or pedestals for the second man to lean on. On one of them he places a model of Ruby as he talks of the perfection of gold. Celeste's punishment for asking these questions is to be followed, since she can no longer be trusted simply to do her job.

Celeste's futile search for answers and Ruby's descent into rabbit-warren-like holes evoke an *Alice in Wonderland*-like reversal of logic and reality. Teresa De Lauretis begins her examination of feminism, semiotics, and cinema, "Alice Doesn't," with a similar comparison to *Through the Looking Glass* and suggests that feminism can learn from this tale that "one must be willing 'to begin an argument,' and so formulate questions that will redefine the context, displace the terms of the metaphors, and make up new ones" (De Lauretis 3). Just such a disturbance seems to be the intention of Celeste. In kidnapping Ruby and questioning the "experts," she begins an argument that shakes the status quo. Having played the roles of meddler, rescuing Ruby and starting her on her quest, and inquisitor, probing the relationship between women and gold, as a dreamer Celeste assumes a further role as a desiring subject with whom we might identify.

The Gold Diggers takes up the closing lament of *Thriller*—that Mimi and Musetta "never got to know each other" and "perhaps . . . would have loved each other." Celeste's quest to settle this problem begins with her opening lines: "Time is short, we have ninety minutes to find each other, to solve this riddle." Once again, Colette is given a voiceover that sets out the trajectory of the film. The first time we see her, she stands against a wall; a shadow of her head is thrown onto the wall, echoing a similar image in *Thriller.*

The "projection" of the double, or the other woman that we find in *Thriller,* is also found in this film. In both films Colette is a curious presence. She might be seen as a standard narrator, setting up the quest narrative of the film, reminding us through her interjections where we are in that quest, searching and finding. Yet in *The Gold Diggers* she is given more subjectivity. She has a desiring dream sequence, a job of sorts, and is active enough to rescue the female hero (twice).

At this early stage, Potter is already using doubles, oppositional females, mirrors, and bisecting narratives in her films. Her use of doubles also comments on their use in mainstream cinema, as Mimi says in *Thriller:* "We were set up as opposites and as complementary characters and kept apart to serve our roles." Celeste and Ruby are opposites in looks and behavior. Celeste dresses in masculine clothes and moves the narrative along. Ruby dresses in feminine clothes, and, emphasized by the casting of Julie Christie, her role is as the object of the gaze. There are two moments when the "togetherness" of Celeste and Ruby is explored, and significantly both rely on dance or choreography as their means of expression. The first moment occurs when Celeste is having a dream, and the second is the ending of the film, when both women have jumped into the water.

Celeste's dream is a prime example of how juxtaposition works in the film. After kidnapping Ruby, Celeste leaves her to go to work, where she questions what she is being asked to do and is then followed home by a group of men. Returning to the hut, Celeste discovers Ruby's absence, but it is as if she then begins to fantasize a different relationship with Ruby.

The fantasy sequence begins with a shot of the now-empty space of the room where Celeste had led Ruby. We see a *Thriller*-like chair, a pair of shoes, and an empty stagelike space dimly lit with a spotlight. We then cut to a completely new space, which appears to be a kind of café. An old lady rises from a table and pulls some curtains back, revealing people on seats facing away from her. Then we cut to two women who are dancing. We cut quickly back to Celeste, whose head is on the pillow, suggesting that the following scenes might be her dream; we cut back to her several times throughout the scene, and she is always sleeping. We then cut between Celeste and Ruby and the women dancing. Celeste and Ruby stand facing each other. In the next shot Celeste is sleeping, and someone (Ruby, it seems) places a hand on her back, caressing her. We see moonlight on water and someone welding on a high platform on a boat. Ruby lifts Celeste to standing position in an embrace.

The two women dancing in a bar are joined by a third woman. All wear trousers with suspenders and have short, androgynous haircuts. A bar woman looks on. We cut from this to a further woman tapping out a beat on some shelves. The spaces seem separate, but the sound becomes the sound track for the three women dancing. This action rises to a crescendo of drumming, finishing with a shot of Celeste sleeping and the old woman returning to her seat, followed by an insert of the welder working on the boat. The sequence ends with a return to the empty space, with chair and shoes, thus safely containing this fantasy of female-to-female desire and equality in the work place.

When the same shot of the welder is used at the end of the film, it recalls this dream sequence, therefore suggesting some of the possibilities of the Ruby/Celeste coupling. Once again, this feminist vision takes place in performance, fantasy, or metaphoric spaces, but the welder should give us some hope that the impact of these isolated attacks on patriarchal domination are being felt in the wider world.

This scene of Celeste dreaming is one of many that suggest a way in which Celeste and Ruby might come together to compensate for Mimi and Musetta never actually becoming friends. While in the film-proper, Celeste has been in command of the action in a traditional male role (rescuing Ruby from the ball, taking her to the cabin, asking her questions, setting the quest in motion), in this dream sequence she is relatively passive, discovered sleeping by Ruby, who first puts her arm across Celeste's back, a sentimental gesture, and then picks her up. The sequences with which this brief dream is intercut might be seen as a poetic expression of the same sentiment. Thus the dancers also enact a movement of coming together and dancing apart, while the quick insert of the woman welding suggests an intervention into a male role.

Thinking of this section in terms of how it might provide pleasure for the female spectator, several possibilities present themselves. We might see the combination of scenes as an example of the expression of femininity as counterposed to its usual repression in classical narrative. Or we might think of it in terms of solidarity among women, from Celeste and Ruby, between whom a relationship is growing to the extent that, as Patricia Mellencamp suggests, "The tale can be read as Ruby's coming out, or coming into lesbian consciousness" (Mellencamp, "Taking" 162). Finally, with its meandering scenes that cross dream, fantasy, dance, and episodic narrative, this section serves as an example of alternative ways of making meaning aside from the standard narrative form, therefore offering an answer to questions posed by feminist film theorists.

Following the *Through the Looking Glass* sequence in which Celeste takes up the position of investigator, seeking answers about the value of money, gold, and the woman, she returns to her cabin to assume the second position: of desiring the heroine. Celeste has disturbed the balance of the narrative world. She has prompted Ruby, the passive heroine, to probe her role and see how much it can be changed if she goes back to her childhood. Celeste has usurped the male heroic role by capturing Ruby and then questioning the authority of the men for whom she works. Therefore, the film's ending can no longer uphold a binary relationship between the two women. Ruby is no longer respectful of her own role. Although she allows herself to be carried, she then behaves mockingly at the dance and is positively delighted when Celeste appears again. The shift in Ruby's consciousness is expressed in her dialogue: "I can project, I am projected. I can repeat, I am repeated. Investors take their place, and I play my part; to the bank with the beauty, to the bank with the gold; both make money, and neither grows old."

As with *Thriller,* the concluding scene is more of an acknowledgment of the undoing of narrative and its roles than a forward-looking conclusion. What is important, Celeste decides, is her consciousness of these processes, her growing revelation as to the impact they have on her life and the continued fight against them. All of this is expressed in the dialogue: "I know that even as I look and even as I see I'm changing what is there." This line is suggestive of Potter's practice in general. Even when she takes "found" texts, references, and genres—*Psycho, La Bohème,* Julie Christie, *Orlando,* the musical, thriller, film noir, costume and historical drama—she transforms them to suit her particular interests. This same line will be useful in considering Potter's next film, *Orlando,* although the term "next" is misleading, since there is a nine-year gap between the two—a gap filled with struggle, heartache, disappointment, and perseverance that proved once again Potter's independence.

Towards Pleasure, Developing Style: *Orlando* and *The Tango Lesson*

The Gold Diggers proves that when Potter looks and sees, she does indeed "change what is there." Her distinctive approach to her material was emerging, yet she still had not fully managed to deal with the problem of pleasure. Potter clearly thinks hard about her audience with each project she approaches. The paradox of her situation is that she wants to make narrative films that show women to be creative, desiring individuals, and she wants her audience to connect with these women; yet she does not want to resort to the patriarchal pleasures associated with classical narrative. For this reason, and influenced by her performance background, she puts together narratives that ask questions and set out quests, that do not have closure, and work through a combination of different elements and threads. These combinations in her first two films challenge and often distance the spectator, who is mostly engaged intellectually and only slightly immersed in the investigations and the combination of sound and image.

Orlando

Potter turned to *Orlando* soon after *The Gold Diggers;* however, it swiftly became apparent that, in light of the confusion and ambivalence met by her previous film, few funders believed that she could adapt Woolf's novel. While finding ways to fund *Orlando,* Potter was also making other projects: a short film, *The London Story* (1986); a four-part television series, *Tears, Laughter, Fear, and Rage* (1986); and a documentary, *I Am an Ox, I Am a Man, I Am a Woman* (1988). Although these projects could be seen as gap-fillers while she was raising money for *Orlando,* each goes some way towards developing elements that would be crucial to the latter film and its success.

In *The London Story,* she took a very simple linear, cause-and-effect narrative and used editing and performances to bring it alive. In *Tears, Laughter, Fear, and Rage,* she used interviews with a variety of people to contemplate the gendered natured of emotions, and for *I Am an Ox, I Am a Man, I Am a Woman,* she visited Russia to research early Russian women filmmakers who had been otherwise forgotten, perhaps continuing her interest in Russian culture that began with her encounter with the Russian avant-garde of the 1920s in her teens, then continued with her visit to the Eisenstein museum in Moscow in 1984.

The London Story is a fifteen-minute short that uses music, dance, action, and intrigue to question Britain's political alliances with America and Europe. Jacky Lansley and George Yiasoumi, both seen in *The Gold Diggers,* star along with Lol Coxhill. The film opens in Whitehall with a low-angle shot looking up at Jacky's face as she takes photos of a doorman and Lol entering the cabinet office. Her surreptitious behavior establishes a spy narrative. We cut to two sequences of degraded handheld footage in which George the doorman and Lol are interviewed. Both are idiosyncratic: while George opens doors and wants to talk of nothing else, the other man is fond of briefcases.

The older man listens to a news broadcast, which fills in the political background to the film. It is vaguely suggested that "the British government" is being pressured to decide their alliances on economic relations with either Europe or the United States and that the future of British industry depends on this. The premise having been set up, we then witness the smuggling of information. The smuggling begins with Jacky, who takes a government minister to the theater and is handed a document by George. Jacky hands this on to Lol, who takes it to a skater at an ice rink. In a hilarious and ridiculous interlude, it is then returned to Jacky by Lol on a bicycle, and she sneaks it into the minister's briefcase. A newscast the following day tells us that there has been a radical U-turn in the government's strategy and that this is an issue of public information. It leaves us with the question, Who are the allies? The film closes with a gentle choreography of movements by the three performers in which Jacky is handed between the two men.

The two documentaries Potter made for television—*Tears, Laughter, Fear, and Rage* and *I Am an Ox, I Am a Man, I Am a Woman*—were commissioned, not initiated by Potter. Both feed into her work to follow. For the latter, Potter's time in Russia led to her eventual collaboration with Lenfilm Studios in St. Petersberg, who provided their facilities, their expertise, and some of the budget for *Orlando*. The former fills the gap between Potter's antinarrative work and her more mainstream productions. It is as if she were rehearsing the role of the emotions in her work. This documentary also pays homage to Michael Powell, who appears in it shortly before his death. It raises the issue of the gendering of emotions, since many of those interviewed comment on how they, as men or women, are expected to react to situations, and how that fits or doesn't fit with how they actually react. Potter has said, "'I think detachment is a virtue. The stereotype of the woman as incapable of detachment comes from the idea that women are closer to the emotions, closer to the dark side—being outside of language in the land of unconscious. A certain kind of misogyny creeps into theoretical language . . . the supposed emotionality of women, the ability to express and discharge feeling, in fact can create a more detached world view'" (qtd. in Cook, "British" 17). Her obvious resistance to men and women being pigeonholed into expected ways of feeling is a key part of her next film.

The London Story was made by Potter with her own money, having been turned down by the BFI and Channel Four. However, once the film was made, Channel Four immediately screened it, its reception was enthusiastic, and the BFI bought it. Although the film is slight, it illustrates Potter's developing style. There is an economy of means and a structure that suits the constraints. Reading the film with her next work in mind, the conflict of Britain, torn between its European partners and forming an alliance with America, is suggestive of the problems the British film industry was undergoing at this time. Ironically, Potter was directly caught up in these problems when trying to find support for *Orlando*.

Orlando was in production for seven years, during which time, according to Christopher Sheppard, "'everyone in the U.K. had turned it down, and potential U.S. partners had all rejected it.'" Consequently, Sheppard writes, "'The only way *Orlando* was going to get made was as a European co-production'" (qtd. in Finney 94). The team that would make it happen only came together in the final four years. Tilda Swinton had worked on the character with Potter, Walter Donohue had filled the role of script editor, and most importantly, Christopher Sheppard became Potter's producer.

It was primarily Sheppard's job to compel others to believe in Potter's vision. That she has still gone in her own direction, rather than relying on critics or studios and money-men, is a tribute to Potter's strength of vision and distinctive creative personality. As if reflecting her struggle, her films depict characters who overcome odds, negotiate conflicts, and seek a hidden truth, a change in society, or a connection with another person. The name of the production company formed for *Orlando,* Adventure Pictures, has proven increasingly apt, as every film Potter has made with this company has been adventurous in form, style, and budget.

Development of the script for *Orlando* was supported by the National Film Development Fund (NFDF) in 1988, a development loan from the European Script Fund (SCRIPT) in 1989, and a second sum from NFDF and then SCRIPT in 1991. By this time Russia's Lenfilm studios had agreed to contribute, and the film had the backing of British Screen, the European Co-production Fund, Mikado Film, Italy, Rio in France, and Sigma in the Netherlands. However, as the film went into preproduction, the French blocked *Orlando*'s application to Eurimages because of Britain's refusal to join the scheme. Christopher Sheppard writes, "'Although *Orlando* had the right percentage splits between its European co-production members to technically qualify, objectors argued that by allowing an essentially British-led project to receive backing was sending the wrong messages to both its own members and the U.K. government'" (qtd. in Finney 94). The only solution to the 20 percent shortfall in the budget was to persuade some of their backers to take delayed repayments (which SCRIPT agreed to do) and for many members of the cast and crew—including Potter and Sheppard—to defer payment of their fees.

This crisis, just before production began, was only one of many that Potter and Sheppard had to deal with in the seven years of *Orlando*'s development and completion. Others included having to remortgage their houses and beg and borrow from friends and relations to make up the $370,000 cost of development, only sixty-six thousand dollars of which was covered by funders. The original $10.6 million budget was cut to $3.8 million, and at the last minute there were costs that couldn't be budgeted for prior to shooting, such as having to make an unofficial payment to local authorities in Uzbekistan, who changed their mind about granting permission to shoot, or covering the costs to reshoot Charlotte Velandrey after she became sick and had to return to Paris early. These meant that ultimately the fees for the director, producer, and company had to be deferred 100 percent.

Ironically, given Potter's struggles with funding in Britain, Pam Cook declares, "[I]ndeed it is a film made by a woman—Sally Potter's *Orlando,* a co-production which wears its dual British/European identity on its sleeve—that suggests a positive way forward for British cinema" (Cook, "Border" xiii). The film's status as a coproduction that made its international partners work for it, and whose pan-European locations feed into a look that is at once about Englishness and at the same time part of a wider European history, makes the film unique and for many a successful case study for further coproductions. Potter's films that follow, while less complex in their production histories, have all been put together as coproductions and similarly cross continents and cultures. The London/Paris locations of *Thriller* and London/Iceland city and landscapes of *The Gold Diggers* must not be forgotten either. Potter's cinema has never located itself purely in England. However, from *Orlando* onwards, her films have used their main protagonists' travel to explore identity as something pertaining not merely to one's sex or gender but also to one's identification of home. *Orlando* initiates this theme, with a main character who seeks to find him/herself "at home." Only after four hundred years, once she has lost the family house and her heritage but produced a book and a child, does she achieve this feeling.

Orlando was premiered at the Venice Film Festival in October 1992. It received a standing ovation and won an OCIC (International Catholic Organization for Cinema and Audio-Visuals) critics award; it went on to win awards at other festivals, a BAFTA, and Oscar nominations for design and makeup. The film was picked up by Sony Pictures Classics and distributed in art-house and mainstream cinemas. Those who knew of Potter's previous work and her struggle to make *Orlando* were typically kind in their assessments of the film. *Screen International* declared, "[F]our years in the making, *Orlando* bursts onto the screen in a blaze of glory" (Dobson 23), while for *The Guardian's* critic Derek Malcolm, the film managed to combine Potter's "previous formalist concerns with a stronger, more vivid grasp of narrative."

Little sign of the struggles that went into the making of *Orlando* is evident on the screen itself. As most reviewers commented, the film has a sumptuousness and fullness of detail that belies its modest budget. Its narrative flows, indeed rushes past masterfully, and conceptually it is one of Potter's most satisfying creations. The most positive reviews of *Orlando* came from critics who judged the film in cinematic terms, as an art-house crowd-pleaser, an enchanting British film by a woman director, or a European coproduction that proves the possibility of artistic success through (or despite) cross-cultural collaboration. Subsequent writing on *Orlando* has also hovered around these subjects, discussing the film's narrative structure and "postmodern" use of costume drama. For Julianne Pidduck, "The ironic costume, gesture, and character movement employed by Potter here highlight issues of gendered physical and social mobility and constraint" (177), while for Cristina Degli-Esposti, adopting a "neo-baroque rereading" of the film, the mise-en-scène is also impressive: "With an abundance of figural representation, Potter's film falls into a particular kind of cinema of excess" (75). For Anne Ciekco, *Orlando* becomes a key film in the debate over national and transnational film production. Its adaptation of Woolf's novel, its casting of iconic British actors and personalities, landscapes, and history all situate it as satirizing Britishness. However, due to the travel across continents that is part of the novel, the coproduction arrangements that brought the film about, and international casting choices (Charlotte

Velandrey, Lothaire Blutheau), *Orlando* can also be seen as a European or transnational film: "Through the staging, writing, and enactment of history and the performance of gender, *Orlando* destabilizes generic categories" (Ciecko, "Transgender" 19).

In terms of its place in cinematic history, *Orlando*'s originality and richness seemed without debate. However, some critics who judged the film as an adaptation of Woolf's novel were less satisfied. While the adaptation of novels for the cinema is common practice, Potter has noted that *Orlando* had been thought to be unadaptable because of its massive scope (its story crosses three centuries), its central conceit (a main character who, for no apparent reason, changes from male to female), and Woolf's playful and ironic style of narration, which depends upon written language for its effect. Potter's answer to these difficulties was to condense, to provide a motivation through plot, and to use direct address, in which Orlando looks into the camera and speaks to the audience.

Orlando raises questions about the differences between literature and film, the written word and the visual image. With regard to the written word, *Thriller* and *The Gold Diggers* display Potter's accomplishment as a wordsmith, featuring intricate scripts containing poems, riddles, and lyrics. The screenplays for *Orlando, The Tango Lesson,* and *The Man Who Cried* showcase Potter's skillful dialogue, and *YES* reinforces her status as a talented writer, with its original and inventive iambic-pentameter verse. As a multimedia polymath who has also written lyrics, it almost goes without saying that Potter was ever aware of the differences between Woolf's written word and any visual interpretation of it.

While quibbling over Potter's editing of Woolf's novel, much discussion among critics revolved around Potter's use of the reverse look as an equivalent to Woolf's self-consciousness and her treatment of the sex-change. Potter's use of the reverse look and of the observer who comments to us derives from her own history of creative practice. In light of this history, Potter's interest in Woolf's novel makes perfect sense.

The novel employs a strikingly self-conscious narrator who is continually digressing from the "action" and commenting on the process of telling the story. Potter's early work was always interested in pointing things out to us, asking us to engage intellectually, and ruminating on the inadequacies of language, so it is appropriate that when she adapts a novel she would choose one that exhibits its insecurities about the conventions of novel writing.

For Pamela Caughie, Woolf's "playful surface" in her novel should be linked to her central ideas: "Language and identity are closely related"; "Just as Orlando's identity swings from the extreme of conventionality to the extreme of eccentricity . . . so the language shifts from the transparent conventionality of clichés . . . to the opaque originality of Orlando and Shel's cipher language" (77–78). Potter's adaptation of *Orlando* tries to find a visual equivalent to this creative use of language and narrative form, and the reverse looks are one way of doing so. The shift in focus to gender identity rather than the formation of a writer is another, as if to visualize Caughie's comment that in the novel "identity is as variable as language, language as vulnerable as identity" (78).

For Suzanne Ferriss and Kathleen Waites, Potter's devices "break . . . the illusion and chang[e] . . . the way we 'read' film, much like Woolf's novel challenges the way we 'read' or understand gender and identity" (111). Perhaps the central transformation from novel to film is the moment where Orlando changes sex. In the novel, this simply happens, with the narrator putting an end to all discussion: "But let other pens treat of sex and sexuality; we quit such odious subjects as soon as we can" (Woolf, *Orlando* 98). In the film, Potter wants her audience to identify with her main character, so she provides a reason: the inability of the male Orlando to fulfill the manly duty of fighting and killing his "enemy."

For Leslie K. Hankins, Potter's treatment of *Orlando* represents a "heterosexualized betrayal of a lesbian love letter" (168). She points to the casting of gay men (Quentin Crisp and Jimmy Sommerville) but laments that "the lesbian presence in the film is conspicuous by its absence" (172). Hankins also critiques Potter's erasure of the female Orlando's relationships with women. However, she restricts her discussion to plot and casting, and although she notes that in the novel "the lesbian narrative is always deferred, suggested, held between the lines" (169), she does not consider the potential for lesbian identification in the exchange of desiring gazes between two women in the scenes between Orlando and Sacha. These scenes offer instances in which the diegetic "male gaze" is troubled, and the actual female-to-female nature of these looks complicates matters even further.

It is clear from its enthusiastic reception that Potter's *Orlando* supplied much pleasure to its audience. Even more evident is the fact that this did not come at the expense of the more serious issues it deals with, from masculinity and femininity as cultural constructions and performances to the social disempowerment of women because of inheritance laws. Orlando, who will be disinherited if she has no son, should be seen alongside Mimi, who, as a poor seamstress, cannot afford to have children, and Ruby, whose value, like gold, is as an exchange mechanism; in herself she has no value. While it is a "crossover" (Lane 96) film, *Orlando* does not abandon Potter's previous concerns or her emerging style.

How, then, does the film make the leap across the "pleasure-time blues" of Potter's early films into the realm of the intelligent *and* entertaining? *Orlando* represents a movement in Potter's practice from the avant-garde to art cinema, overtly feminist politics of sexual difference to a more humanist assertion of "same person, different sex," and complex counter-cinema strategies to a simpler, classical narrative structure.

In *Orlando,* some of the sketchiness of Potter's early films is filled in. We have "real" set design rather than performance spaces and geographically and historically definable places rather than mythic or dreamlike spaces. Rather than the film being structured around a quest to find out the truth behind a story ("Was I murdered?") or to connect two characters ("We have ninety minutes to find each other"), *Orlando* tells a story that advances through time in which the main protagonist meets a variety of people and develops and undertakes a journey that reaches an end. The film's images, passages to the illusionism, are sumptuous and stunning to look at, and intricate camera work and editing comment on the story.

However, this description of the more conventional elements of *Orlando* fails to account for the narration. In novel and film, the moment when Orlando changes sex is downplayed, and the extraordinary nature of the tale is deferred into the way that it is told. In her telling, Potter uses elements recognizable from her early work: an observer figure to guide us through and comment on the action and an episodic structure, here through the interruption posed by the intertitles. This is combined with self-conscious camera movement, brusque editing, key musical themes, and an emphasis on artifice through performances, costumes, and settings—all of which disrupt the illusion that is otherwise created.

Despite its art-cinema flavor, *Orlando* opens with the same kind of attempt to connect with its audience that is found in *Thriller* and *The Gold Diggers*. While in the earlier two films, Colette Laffont invites us to solve first a riddle and then a "murder," in *Orlando* we are directly addressed by the protagonist, who indicates that the narration will be self-conscious and playful, drawing us in and addressing us directly. Like Colette/Mimi, the dialogue shifts persons to indicate that Swinton is playing a part. Colette/Mimi shifts from the third person—"They do what they can for her, but Mimi dies"—to the first person ("Is this the story of my life?"), as she begins to retell the story from Mimi's point of view. Similarly, Swinton's "narrator," whom we do not meet again, begins in third person: "There can be no doubt about his sex—despite the feminine appearance that every young man of the time aspires to. And there can be no doubt about his upbringing. Good food, education, a nanny, loneliness, and isolation. And because this is England, Orlando would therefore seem destined to have his portrait on the wall and his name in the history books. But when he"—at which point, the onscreen Orlando turns to look to the camera and declares, "That is, I," then looks away again as the narration continues—"came into the world, he was looking for something else. Though heir to a name which meant power, land, and property, surely when Orlando was born it wasn't privilege he sought, but company."

Colette's shift in person begins an acting-out of the *La Bohème* story and is therefore an evident getting-into-role that is in keeping with the performance space of the attic. Although Orlando's similar shift in person is not so abrupt, since "he" is already "in role," in the opening image of the film there is the same sense of a performance being put on, as evidenced in the camera movement, editing, and dialogue. The opening shot frames Orlando in a field of long grass beneath a tall tree. He is already pacing from left to right, but the camera is still for a few seconds. Then the camera also begins to move, but it does so in the opposite direction to Orlando. Though its movements are contrary, they are also in time with Orlando's own. As he moves, the camera moves; as he pauses, the camera hesitates; as he paces back, the camera tracks once more. It is almost as if Orlando and the camera are playing a game together, suggesting a closeness between camera and character.

The narration begins after the first complete track from left to right, at which point the sound of Orlando's rehearsal of his poem is turned down so that we can hear the intimate voiceover. We continue to look at Orlando pacing until the narrator says, "Orlando would therefore seem destined to have . . . ." Orlando is sitting under the oak tree, and we cut to a close-up on his face. He looks off right, yet his look is not the subjective or contemplative one we might expect. Instead, at the moment that Orlando interjects, "That is, I," the swift darting of his eyes towards the camera makes it apparent that he has been listening to the narrator and therefore aware that he is being looked at.

We cut to a wider shot as the narrator says, "Though heir to a name," and we see Orlando pick up a piece of blank parchment and a quill. Then, as the narrator says, "but company," we cut back to a close-up on Orlando's hands with his quill poised above the parchment. He returns it to the ground, and we cut back to his face; his eyes, at first looking down at the page, are then raised, though they still do not look at us.

Orlando's shift from third-person narrator to speaking subject raises the possibility that this opening sequence should be seen retrospectively as the opening of the book Orlando will write. If we take this to be the case, then *Orlando* can be seen to possess the same kind of circular narrative as *Thriller*. This first look to camera is a reverse look that shatters the "fourth wall," which ensures that characters remain

From the beginning of *Orlando*, the reverse look
is established. © Adventure Pictures Ltd.

unaware of our spectatorship. Our position as anonymous voyeurs is guaranteed by this rule. However, such conventions work alongside a conception of the privileged position of the spectator and the powerful "patriarchal" camera. As we've seen with Potter's earliest film, *Jerk*, she has always rejected the powerful and seamless kind of direction because of its effect on power relationships inside the frame, between bodies in space, and outside the frame, between the audience and the film. *Orlando* attempts to connect us intimately with the main character. In her introduction to the published screenplay, Potter writes that the look back is "a golden thread that would connect the audience, through the lens, with Orlando, and in this way the spectacle and the spectator would become one through the release of laughter" (Potter, *Orlando* xiii). Although we do not laugh at every look Orlando casts at us, the fact that with each he extracts himself from the fiction to share something with us implies the connection Potter suggests.

While the reverse look invites an intimacy and reciprocity between Orlando and the audience, the tone and content of the voiceover undercuts this slightly. We have several seconds to view Orlando before the narration begins. In these seconds, whether we recognize Tilda Swinton or not, we may have been wondering if this character is male or female. Therefore, when the narrator begins matter of factly, "There can be no doubt about his sex," the image and/or our extratextual knowledge contradict this statement. The line that follows ("Despite the feminine appearance that every young man of the time aspires to") sets up femininity and masculinity as indefinite categories that don't necessarily have anything to do with one's sex. The uncertainty that this opening image and narration creates is somewhat relieved by Orlando's first look back, which, as well as establishing a connection, asks us to suspend our disbelief and begins the process of asking us to relate to an essence rather than an appearance. The look back at the camera and these opening lines together reinforce our complicity in the illusionism of the story. Since there clearly are doubts about Orlando's sex when we first see "him," the narration should be seen as ironic, and this tone is confirmed later by the description of Orlando's upbringing: "Good food, education, a nanny"—all of which seem usual—joined by "loneliness and isolation." The look back might also be seen as a plea to serve as company.

The reflexivity of the opening of *Orlando,* which invites us to be inside and outside at the same time, is in keeping with the "exteriorization of consciousness" that Potter has spoken of as the predominant style in Woolf's novel. We must get used to watching and experiencing with Orlando, seeing events and then hearing Orlando's thoughts about them. While such a viewing position might be thought of as an identification with and then a distancing from a character, we are never fully tied in with Orlando; ours is a relationship that must grow over time. Time is obviously important to the narrative, since over time Orlando learns the problems of identification as a man and a woman, finds company (however briefly), and succeeds in creating his/her novel.

The structure of *Orlando* is accumulative, as every new stage, marked with an intertitle, suggests a moving on and equally a moving away from what has gone before. The opening untitled scenes act as the prologue, introducing us to Orlando. This is followed by "1600 DEATH," "1610 LOVE," "1650 POETRY," "1700 POLITICS," "1750 SOCIETY," "1850 SEX," and finally "BIRTH." The picaresque nature of these episodes is suggested by the heavy issues of the titles. The film does not hesitate in jumping from one stage to the next, and this is matched by the speed at the heart of the mise-en-scène. Orlando begins the film at speed. In his lateness for a royal appointment, he is running from boyhood leisure into a world of responsibility and parental and societal rules. This initial fleeing continues as a metaphor for aging and the passing of time. Following the queen's visit, which opens the film, the next sequence begins with a slowly walking funeral procession, as Orlando buries his mother shortly after the offscreen death of his father. In "1610 LOVE," which is largely set on ice, we have scenes with groups walking and skating. In "1650 POETRY," Orlando runs behind the poet Green, who tries to blackmail the vulnerable young poet into guaranteeing him a pension. In "1700 POLITICS," after arriving in Khiva in central Asia on a swaying camel, Orlando walks with a group of twinned men to meet the Khan.

The episode titled "1750 SOCIETY" begins with a distressed servant following Orlando across the lawn and warning her about taking up the invitation to the poets and ends with Orlando running from Archduke Harry through the maze and out onto moorland. Finally, "1850 SEX" ends with a pregnant Orlando running across a battlefield through muddy puddles. Only in "BIRTH" is walking or running replaced by a motorbike and a distinct lack of haste. In none of these scenes is there any significant geographical travel going on, but psychological developments in Orlando's search for company are suggested. Thus the Khan, Greene, the poets, and Harry all want something from Orlando and also offer different ways of performing the self, as English ambassador, poet or benefactor, muse or poet, and object of desire.

Throughout this whirlwind tour of history, each episode is crowded with detail and filled with sumptuous colors and movement. Like the walking motif that keeps history moving, a series of theatrical effects and performances ensure that each episode is colorful and entertaining. The first effect is the aside to camera that operates like a soliloquy in the theater. Orlando does not actually speak to us, but his/her looks definitely communicate his/her feelings about a person at a given moment. There are thirteen of these looks to camera, some accompanied by dialogue and others not. Orlando seeks something different in each.

Theatricality is also present through the over-the-top settings and costumes, in which each era is crowded with detail and filmed with sumptuous colors and movement. There is something ostentatious about Orlando's costumes. Often they match a particular setting. For example, when he goes to see the queen, her striped bed linen is matched by Orlando's striped top. As the Brontëesque heroine, circular patterns in Orlando's headdress are repeated on her shoulders. In each era there are performances and ceremonies going on, from Orlando's recitation to the queen to the dancers on the ice, the creation of the tableau vivant, the peasants playing with poles, and the fireworks.

If we include the many moments of singing—from Jimmy Sommerville singing for the queen and the woman in Uzbek to the man singing for the poets and the closing "angel"—then the quota of performance matches her two previous films, both of which included dance sequences and song. However, the effect is different here. In *Thriller,* the opera is used as an example of the kind of hyperbolic text within which Colette can find no place, while the "dancing" is a way of reinforcing the place of the past in the present and finding an equivalent, such as when "Mimi" says that she was carried out "in arabesque, yes that's right, in arabesque." The "perfection" of the arabesque position (which relies on the support of a partner and yet is heralded not for the work of the partner but for the perfection of the dancer's technique as she bends herself into a strain position) says something particular about the "feminine" in the same way that Mimi's fate, prescribed as it is from the beginning of the opera, also speaks of working-class femininity and suffering. Orlando's true love, Shelmerdine, asserts, "If I was a woman . . . I might choose not to sacrifice my life caring for my children, nor my children's children. Nor to drown anonymously in the milk of female kindness. But instead, say, to go abroad," whereas Colette/Mimi in *Thriller* realizes that the suffering woman is her sole function in the drama.

The repetition of theatrical and performance elements throughout Potter's films is accompanied by the development of her cinematic style, including her use of camera and editing, mise-en-scène, and narrative. Potter has spoken in interviews of wanting to get a balance in *Orlando,* to depict history without striving for authentic details. The film's disrespectful and playful tone is set by Orlando's asides. However, an even more powerful force in upholding this tone is the camera movement, which offers a reinforcing gesture of irony. Therefore, the sets may have been dressed to maximum decorative effect, using parallel lines and renaissance perspective, yet the camera disrespects these lines and decenters many of its shots.

The first example of the undercutting camera is in the opening scene. Tracking in the opposite direction to Orlando, the camera's height is relatively low; we can see the long grass in front of him. The movement of the camera immediately inserts a self-conscious element into the scene, along with the voiceover, which draws attention to our look at Orlando, and the invitation to share his space and thoughts when no one else is around. The movement of the camera is not the masterly one we might associate with the tracking shots in the films of someone like Peter Greenaway, with which *Orlando* shares the distinctive production design of Ben Van Os and Jan Roelfs and is therefore often compared. The camera's movement is casual; it does not "float" ethereally. As it tracks, we can see that the ground is bumpy. The long grass moves, and as the camera stops moving in one direction, it seems to hesitate uncertainly. The camera draws attention to itself: it does not give us seamless framing; it moves around, reframes, and follows; it intervenes. In all these aspects it reflects Potter's avant-garde impulse within this more mainstream subject and treatment.

At other moments, the camera cuts against the immaculate design of the sets through a series of repeated movements and treatments. The next recurrent camera movement that we encounter after the opening is a kind of zig-zag track in which the camera first crosses left to right and then shifts to cross right to left. This occurs during two encounters: the first is when Orlando, late, runs into the crowded hall to take a bowl of rose-petal water to the queen; and the second is in "1850 SEX," in Orlando's bed space as she walks around a table to Shelmerdine, carrying a bowl of milk for a drink. In both cases the camera goes against the formal lines of the mise-en-scène and other bodies present in the frame.

Given the subject matter, in these cases the camera could be seen to express the power relationships between the tardy Orlando and the queen, or Orlando and her emerging object of desire, Shelmerdine, whom Orlando will wait on and then possess. Had these scenes been filmed with a static camera and a shot that showed the entire space from the beginning, the dynamics of power would not have been so apparent. In the scene with Shelmerdine, it is as if the carrying of the bowl of milk is a journey in itself. Orlando must walk around a long wooden table unencumbered by the ridiculously large skirts she's worn in earlier scenes—as if she has grown into her femininity. In the earlier scene, we see her run up the main aisle and skirt around some flower arrangements to find her parents, from whom she collects the bowl of rosewater and then continues in a straight line to finish kneeling before the queen.

The similarity of these scenes, brought to our attention by the camera movements, begs a comparison between the gestures that Orlando makes to the queen and then to her prospective lover. Both are important figures in her history, since both express their love for her and give her something—a house and then a child (we presume the girl is Shelmerdine's, although it is not explicitly indicated). The queen's insistence that Orlando not grow old and Shelmerdine's gift of a child guarantee Orlando's longevity. In terms of his/her longing for company, these encounters are the most genuine of all, although the power relations are reversed as we go from the first to the second.

On meeting Elizabeth I, Orlando acts as a young courtier, answering the queen's every whim. His innocence and youth are emphasized by his association with water; as he hands her the rosewater bowl, we see a shot–reverse-shot from the face of the queen to that of Orlando. While the shadow of the queen's hair over her face makes it dark and could associate her with death, on Orlando's the rosewater makes patterns that bleach out his skin even further.

Later, Orlando follows the queen around the gardens; she ties a garter around his leg and then requires him to come and see her in her bedroom. Here we see the queen take off her day garments and lie on her bed. She calls Orlando to "come"; disengaging from the queen, he looks apprehensively at the camera before approaching her bed. In front of the fire, so that crackling flames play across the scene, the queen beckons to Orlando to sit on her bed and then gives him the decree, taking his face in her hands before instructing him not to wither or grow old.

In the scene with Shelmerdine, the earlier appearance of youthful innocence is replaced by dark colors that contrast with Orlando's pale skin. Orlando's eyes are now dark pupils of brown and black, and this is echoed in a necklace with similar black circles. This darkness picks up Shelmerdine's dark hair, eyes, and clothes, and once again the scene takes place next to a fire.

Orlando brings a bowl for drinking and hands it to Shelmerdine, kneeling in front of him. She bends to pour some hot water from a kettle into a larger bowl, and we cut from the kettle being poured to Orlando's face looking down. Although the position from which we look at Orlando does not match exactly with that of Shelmerdine, it is meant to be his look at Orlando; this is a different kind of look at her than we have encountered before. We notice her rising bosom and the swaying of her necklace. Once she looks up at him, we see the way in which her eyes match the black circles of her necklace and earrings. We cut between Orlando and Shelmerdine as they look at each other and talk of his profession: "the pursuit of liberty." Then the camera begins to pan from one to the other, a movement it makes more than once in the film. The first time occurs when Orlando meets the Khan in Khiva, and it is followed by the scene between Orlando and the poets in "1650 POETRY." These previous times seem engineered to suggest awkwardness between the characters, which is absent from this later scene.

As Orlando and Khan drink to each other, we pan back and forth between them. The use of a continuous pan rather than sharp cuts means that the duration of the drinking is fully felt, and the awkwardness of the encounter and actual space between the two characters is also captured. In the second example, the poets have gestured to Orlando to sit down in front of them. She does so, and we cut to behind her head as they begin to disparage "woman." The pan takes us to either end of the seated poets and prevents us from seeing Orlando's face until the verbal sparring ends, and we cut back around to witness her dismay. In this case, the pan is less about showing the spatial arrangement of characters than about complementing the poetic dialogue, which is uninterrupted. Since the pan is from behind Orlando's head, and we are denied a reaction shot from her until the end, it also seems as if their remarks are directed more widely than simply at her.

The half-moon pan in the scene with Shelmerdine takes place across a conversation about shifting the roles that men and women should play. Orlando begins by asking Shelmerdine how he fights for freedom and insists that if she were a man she might choose not to fight. Shelmerdine replies that she would not be a real man. He then insists that if he were a woman, he would not sacrifice everything for his children; she asks if he would then be a real woman. The pan takes us from one face to the other in an extreme close-up, a movement that binds these people together as if they are speaking the same words. The impression of two minds meeting explains Orlando's reaction, which is to passionately clasp Shelmerdine to her, thus meeting mental closeness with physical closeness.

These repetitive panning movements become opportunities for us to assess Orlando's encounters with other people. Substituting temporal continuity for the juxtaposition we might otherwise get from shot–reverse-shots, they show the physical awkwardness, discomfort, and overwhelming nature of these encounters and ultimately remind us that those closest to Orlando are not a part of the fiction: those with whom he shares confidences (the audience). The series of three panning sequences, like the zig-zag camera movements, punctuate the film with comparable moments that mark key points in Orlando's journey. Whether we compare Queen Elizabeth and Shelmerdine, or the encounter with Khan, the poets, then Shelmerdine again, each of these moments seem to be meant as an advance on "company."

Orlando's encounter with Shelmerdine almost threatens to break the mold of solitude that has been set around him/her. However, she cannot resist telling us, "I think I'm going to faint. I've never felt better in my life," thereby renewing the hierarchy of confidences in our favor.

In terms of Potter's practice thus far, though, Shelmerdine deserves recognition as a radical hero. Unlike Rodolpho and the other artists and poets, or the men who dance with and then chase Ruby or obstruct Celeste, Shelmerdine understands Orlando. This is apparent from their first conversation, when she says that she does not even know his name, though she feels she knows everything about him, and he says that is what happens when like meets like.

Although the opening of *Orlando* and the many reverse looks that follow interrupt the flow of the narrative and ensure that cracks appear in the illusion, in the moments when the story flows we witness a more fully rounded character. For the first time in Potter's oeuvre, in *Orlando* we meet a character (rather than a performer) who is allowed to desire, and whose desire we witness onscreen. Whereas *Thriller* is the story of Mimi rejecting her place in the tragic narrative, in which there seems to be no place to explore her desire, and *The Gold Diggers* finds only female partners for its protagonists, in *Orlando* we are witness to his pursuit of Sacha and her affair with Shelmerdine.

This is also the first Potter film in which we encounter the male gaze; it would be followed by Pablo in *The Tango Lesson*, César in *The Man Who Cried*, and then HE in *YES*. In all of these films the men look uneasily, and desire is matched by other emotions. In *Orlando* the difficulty of gazing is most pronounced; this is not the all-mastering gaze that characterizes male desire in mainstream film.

The awkwardness of Orlando's desire, his vulnerability and powerlessness once in its thrall, is emphasized by the many close-ups on his face. The first close-up we have of Orlando contrasts his innocent, youthful face with that of the queen. This is followed by an extreme close-up, again a reverse shot from the queen's face once she has stopped him from reciting his poem; this time he looks confused, and we see him swallow nervously. In the next scene the queen's revelation as she puts a garter on his leg—that he will stay in England, the son of her old age—is played through an extreme close-up of Orlando looking up with uncertainty.

This accumulation of Orlando's visage represents him as innocent, young, and vulnerable and very much at the mercy of the queen, due to her seniority in years and position. The funeral of Orlando's mother, where we are given only a side view of him, is followed by a moment when he faces the camera with his fiancée as if for a portrait, standing underneath the portrait of his parents. We next encounter his gaze on the ice, once he catches sight of Sacha. Orlando skates next to his fiancée, then looks to the side and sees Sacha skating confidently around her father and his men. To stand and look, Orlando extracts himself from his fiancée and positions himself next to the Earl of Moray, as if his desiring gaze needs the company of another man to strengthen it. Both stare at Sacha as her party are presented to the host. As Moray turns away, Orlando moves closer and stares harder, transfixed.

Later, at supper in a tent, Orlando sits on the end of a table with that same look on his face. He and Sacha talk and are filmed using equally extreme close-ups. The vulnerability that was present in Orlando's face in the company of the queen remains, as he looks down slightly to Sacha, but his bare face contrasts sharply with hers, lined with the fur from her hat. While she turns her head slightly to listen to the host telling a joke to her father, Orlando remains facing forward, flattened by the lack of contrasting shadows and thrusting, as if trying to pierce her with his gaze.

The centerpiece of Orlando's desiring gaze follows the meal. A stately dance begins, for which the couples line up in the middle while Sacha and her partner skate around in a circle. As Orlando's friends chide him for his pursuit of a "cossack" at the expense of every English woman in the land, he becomes increasingly absorbed in the circling Sacha and increasingly exhibitionist in following her with his gaze. However, the pattern of the dancing makes it difficult for him to look elsewhere and follow Sacha, since he is surrounded by other dancers, and it is hard for him to see beyond their lines. Ultimately, he breaks rank completely and, looking backwards when he should be looking forwards, skates on bended knee out of the circle and across to Sacha, who encircles him more directly as he declares his love for her. Gazing and desiring are shown to be difficult, censored by society and Orlando's position—a public act through which Orlando becomes increasingly conspicuous and that is not as easy or conventional as one might expect. This still-vulnerable gaze will later be contrasted with the equality between Orlando and Shelmerdine in which, although both are framed equally, Shelmerdine's role as patient, having twisted his ankle, could either be seen as forcing Orlando into a caring role or allowing her to be more active in the seduction.

Looking at *Orlando's* playful translation of the novel's self-conscious style, we can see how this film overcame the pleasure-time blues of Potter's early work. By creating an illusionist diegetic world that is also broken with (through the reverse look, camera movement, and editing) and added to (through the performance elements), Potter combines the entertaining and the critical. The film remains her biggest success and at one point was even the highest-selling film at the British box office. Further, and most important, the disengagement that is encouraged in Potter's first two films is present in a very different way here, as the film ends with the utopian suggestion that Orlando has been able to let go of the past because she has assured her place in the future with the birth of her daughter. Creativity and company are the conflicting lines through the narrative, and they find their way into *The Tango Lesson*.

The Tango Lesson

Following the critical and commercial success of *Orlando*, it would have been easy for Potter to put the years of struggling behind her and take one of the many *Orlando*-like projects that were being offered to her. Instead, she took the time to develop her own ideas (including a first draft of *The Man Who Cried*) and took time out from writing to learn the tango to a professional level. Inevitably, perhaps, she came back to the cinema.

If some of the challenge of adapting *Orlando* had to do with the visualizing of Woolf's prose, in *The Tango Lesson* Potter had to find external ways of expressing the personal effects of the tango on the body. Choreography, camera, and editing combine to inscribe the audience in the passionate space that Sally discovers in her most successful moments of dancing. What is most surprising about her success in dancing is that it opens up a feminine space that Sally grows to like. However, the central partnership between Sally (Potter, as herself) and Pablo (Pablo Veron), with its jostling of egos, problematizes this feminine space by reminding her that in relaxing, enjoying, and letting go, in following her desire, she also relinquishes some control.

The contrast between the dancing Sally loves and the directing role that she cannot let go of might be seen as one between femininity and feminism. Lucy Fischer contrasts the trials of the screenplay Sally is writing in the film with the joys of the tango she discovers thus: "[I]n trekking around the world in pursuit of the tango, she chooses pleasure over pain——an amorous 'last tango in Paris' rather than a grim 'dance of death'" (Fischer 44). This contrast is figured in the film as one between being in front of the camera (seen) and being behind it (seer). The division of roles assumed by Sally in the film and Potter in real life reminds us of the repeated undecidability throughout much of Potter's work. She can't choose whether to dance or film, whether to give herself up to and partner with Pablo or remain in control and look at him. Through her indecision, her audience is also repeatedly given choices.

The choices we are allowed in Potter's films are suggestive of the space she leaves for us to complete them. However, some of the looseness of structure in *The Tango Lesson* is also expressive of Potter's improvisational approach to the creative process. Towards the end of the film, when Pablo and Sally walk in a park and plan—or disagree over—the film she will cast him in, there comes a moment when we wonder where we are in the creative process: we have been watching a film made by her with him in it, yet now they are talking about how they would make that film. There is a circularity to *The Tango Lesson* that is reminiscent of *Thriller* and *Orlando.* But at that moment, when we seem to be caught in the film within the film, the completeness of creation that we are used to encountering unravels, and we are at once with Potter in the present moment of creation and with Sally looking forward to the future delivery of the film.

"You can't really film the experience of dancing, at least not directly. You may get the surface of it, but you don't get anything that resembles the incredible feeling in the body that dance gives you" (MacDonald, "Interview" 195). Potter's words are taken from an interview with Scott Macdonald two years prior to the release of *The Tango Lesson* in which she tells him that she was been out tangoing all night. This conversational mention of what she has been doing in her spare time indicates the autobiographical and almost accidental nature of *The Tango Lesson.*

A later article reiterates Potter's all-consuming preoccupation with learning tango at the time: "If I love dance *this much,* does this mean I should be a dancer? Can I be a serious film-maker *and* whiz off to Buenos Aires to dance the nights away?" (Potter, "Gotta Dance" 298). This soul searching finds its way into the film as an exploration of how Sally can give herself up to her tango partner "fifty-fifty" (297) when as a director she is so used to being in charge. The sexual politics of such partnerships is also scrutinized. As if in recognition of Potter's passion for the tango, *The Tango Lesson* marks a shift in Potter's practice as it fully addresses female desire. This shift can be explored further through a focus on our identification with Sally and her gaze, Pablo's narcissism, and the power struggle between the two that transforms into a spiritual yearning to be "at home" with each other.

The Tango Lesson returns to some of the questions around the dancing body raised by Potter's first two films: ideals of femininity, the power relationship between partners, the evocation of the couple in the dancing pair, and the playing out of romance and fantasy through dance. However, there are also developments from those films. Mimi is a victim whose fate is dictated by narrative need. Ruby's future is wide open, but we cannot conceive of a man who might fulfill her once Celeste has opened her eyes. *Orlando* finds her partner only by changing sex and therefore being able to empathize with men. In contrast, Sally and Pablo are a couple for whom opportunities are wide open. At times both are constructed as objects of desire, both control the power at different points, and both also look, although in different ways.

The importance of Sally's gaze at Pablo and the world is established in the opening sequence, before the start of the twelve lessons that divide the narrative in Potter's customary episodic way. Unable to find inspiration for the film she is writing, Sally leaves her bare room and wanders through the city. She is drawn by music to a packed theater, where she witnesses the end of Pablo's tango dance with his partner. As she enters the theater, it is at first hard to see Sally; we barely make her out among the crowds of bodies watching the show. Soon, though, she finds a space between other lookers and, leaning her arm on a low wall, places her chin on her hand. A look of fascination immediately lights up her face. The camera gives us a reverse shot of what she is looking at: Pablo dancing. She remains fascinated, with a slight smile appearing across her lips.

In terms of Laura Mulvey's dismal prediction for the female spectator—that she is only ever the object to be looked at and never the one to look or, by implication, express her desires—Potter's gaze seems a world away. Her gaze follows its subject intently; it also seems full of desire. Potter's face lights up from her voyeuristic position in the dark looking at the dancing images on the screen.

In Sally's delighted first look at Pablo, the creation
of an idea and the creation of an attraction
coexist. © Adventure Pictures Ltd.

Reading backwards from the film that unfolds, this opening moment
reveals the particularities of this female desire: Potter adores Pablo
most, desires him most, and loves him most when she can be simply allowed to look, as if from behind a camera. His performances throughout
the film place her in this camera-position. Significantly, it is only once
she strays to the other side, as the female protagonist rather than the
spectator, that things start to go wrong. The paradox of the tango—that
one can never externalize the feeling of the dancing, even though those
movements are expressive and melodramatic—seems to be reflected
in Sally's plight. As a protagonist (dancer), she can never really feel in
control of her emotions; but as a looker (director), she can fully express
her feelings through her art.

With this opening, we are drawn into Sally's mind, clearly suggesting
that she might become some sort of identification point for us. For the
rest of the film, she assumes the familiar position of observer, familiar
first from Colette Laffont's place and then that of Orlando. Each of these
women stands aside to some extent and looks on, and this position will be
adopted next by Christina Ricci as Suzie in *The Man Who Cried*. What
do we make of these sometimes passive observers in Potter's cinema?
For one, they add a dimension of reflexivity to her dramas. We have

someone's comment on events as they occur, even if simply through a look, as in *Orlando*. They also offer a point of connection to the spectator, a place from which he or she can view.

We spend a lot of time in *The Tango Lesson* watching Sally looking. Having left her office to scout for locations in Paris, we witness her pacing out shots that we later see created in color. For example, she stands at the foot of some stone steps and then walks up and down them slowly, looking around carefully. Later we see the three models precariously balanced on these steps and descending; one is shot and falls to the bottom. We also see Potter walking then running alongside a hedge. She bends so that the top of the hedge is at eye level, then places her hand on top and measures out steps. When we are shown the fully realized shot, it becomes evident that Sally was placing herself in the position of the camera, which tracks along at the same height while the designer with no legs pulls himself along on his hands. Sally's personification as camera prepares us for Pablo's later accusation that she is not really with him; she is merely looking at him, like a camera.

Her looking position takes on other meanings at different moments throughout the film. It is from her delighted gaze at Pablo that the narrative begins. She must then continue to watch and learn and take things in so as to progress as a tango dancer. However, the majority of her learning is undertaken by feeling her way, being with a partner, moving with his body, and being encouraged to undertake different moves in relation to him. The division between looking and not dancing and feeling or dancing with a partner is key. This is perhaps the reason why the climax of Sally's dancing occurs not with Pablo but with the various men in the salon, following her lessons with the two dancers, men she doesn't wish to look at but only to dance with. It is clear from the camera's movement and the reaction of the teachers that a transformation is going on, as the external (the clever steps as seen from outside) and internal (the weight of the bodies against each other, the transformation of body through music) meet and mingle briefly. Here the faces and bodies show the emotion described in the music in a one-off meeting of mind and body. From this point on, Sally seems to know the tango from the inside. This is underlined when she is in the taxi for the second time and the driver comments on the music from his radio as being only understandable if one has loved and lost; then he asks her if she has a boyfriend. In silent reply, Sally daydreams out the window on which rain falls, a classic shot of interiority that suggests that, yes, she has loved and lost or loved and suffered and has experienced this as part of her dancing.

The first time we see Pablo, it is through Sally's eyes. The delight on her face as he dances suggests that she has found something that will be significant to her. Unlike the previous scene in which we registered only frustration, as the scenario of "Rage" played out in her head and onscreen, here we see ideas engendered. Something is born when Sally witnesses Pablo dance. The creation of an idea and the creation of an attraction, a pull towards another, coexist at this important moment.

To pursue her idea, Sally must get closer to Pablo; therefore, the company that she has to reject in order to work in her bare room is part of this alternative creative process. However, the relationship with Pablo is complicated by an attraction on both sides. Thus, once she approaches him, Sally's attractiveness is tentatively established. Following this show, we see Pablo in a bar being hailed by adoring friends, while along one wall sits Sally looking on. She stands and approaches him and tries to tell him, in French, how much she enjoyed the performance, how he was "comme un acteur dans un film." His disinterested tolerance of her praise shifts entirely when she mutters these words. He asks if she works in cinema; she replies "yes" and asks if he gives tango lessons. A wide shot of these exchanges allows us to see the crowd behind the two, and we observe Pablo's dance partner looking Sally up and down, her demeanor suggesting that she is threatened by Sally's advance.

Despite the suggestion that Sally could become an object of some-one's desire, Pablo is the only character who does not look at her. The main reason for this is his own narcissism. Aware of the fact that it was his performance on stage that brought Sally to him, he seems unable to adopt any role in relation to her other than performer. This tendency is expressed through the use of various mirrors that gradually show the way that Pablo has to look at himself to see her.

The first time we encounter this Pablo/mirror theme is when he has begun a routine around his flat. Following tap dances with lettuce and juggling with tomatoes, he jumps up onto the fireplace, where he taps and twirls while watching himself in the large mirror above it. The scene is shot to show, once again, Sally's fascination at seeing him perform, and they have been having a conversation about what he might do in her film. Even so, his behavior seems conspicuously narcissistic, and his look through the mirror says, "I'm looking at you looking at me."

This scene bears comparison with *Thriller,* in which Colette tells us she sat in front of the mirror "waiting for a clue." However, the image we see framed from behind her head is not of her face but a repetition of the back of her head. Looking in the mirror only seems to deepen the mystery. The same could be said for *The Gold Diggers,* in which the metaphor of the looking glass is evoked through the Alice-type activities that ensue once Celeste begins to look for answers to her questions, or once Ruby tumbles into rooms that hold her past, her present, and fantasy scenes. The message from these first two films seems to be that women can gain nothing from the looking glass. In *Orlando* the emphasis is slightly different, as the view from the mirror confirms to Orlando and us that he has indeed changed into a she. Rather than a dissembler, the mirror is the sight of a truth that we need to be convinced of to appreciate why Orlando is treated as she is.

The mirror in *The Tango Lesson* operates in between these previous uses. Pablo looks in the mirror to check that Sally is still looking at him and to invite the praise of the audience. We could compare Pablo's mirror looks to Orlando's looks at camera, since both seek confirmation of their audience's presence and involvement with their current action. However, Orlando's look towards us is not also a look at herself; hers is a one-way mirror in which she wants to see only us, whereas Pablo's look requires a look at himself and at his audience watching him. In short, he wants to be sure that he is watched.

Pablo's narcissistic tendencies can be excused because he is a dancer and because they fit the familiar, culturally accepted masculine behavior identified by critics over the past twenty years. As a dancer, the looker/looked at dyad is one that Pablo lives through on a daily basis. Despite the film's distance from Potter's early work, Pablo's reflexive qualities comment on some of her earliest preoccupations, explored in *Hors d'oeuvres,* about human gestures and when and how they might be altered by becoming part of a dance. Pablo's behavior also fits the narcissistic attitude towards dress and accessorizing identified by Suzanne Moore in her 1988 essay on the emerging "new man."

But to return to the coupling of Sally and Pablo, how does the balance of power shift once this new male attitude is incorporated? The partnership clearly begins with an exchange. In that first conversation, Pablo's eager question, "Do you work in cinema?" is met with Sally's equally keen, "Do you give tango lessons?" Each wants something from the other, and there is no pretense otherwise. The power that Sally may have through her part of the bargain is not, however, immediately evident. In the first lesson Pablo is assertive, while she is permissive. As her critical teacher, he manipulates her, moves her back and forth roughly, instructs her to find her axis, holds her chin, and makes her raise her head high.

The force of Pablo's actions is revealed only when we see Sally with the other two men, Gustavo (Gustavo Naveira) and Fabián (Fabián Salas). With them she seems far more relaxed; they play with her, hold her gently, and guide her—they seem to consider her a delicate body. After Pablo and Sally's first proper public dance, which seems to go well, the partnership is reaffirmed as he says that he's always wanted be in films, and she says that she always wanted to be a dancer. However, he soon establishes limits on their dance/real-life relationship: they rehearse, and he keeps telling her to let go. He keeps stopping but tells her that it is she who keeps stopping. After their unfulfilling performance, he says that she must give up all idea of what it is to be strong onstage: "Just follow, otherwise you block my freedom." She says he dances like a soloist. Then, in their emotional conversation over the phone she tells him: "All you're interested in is being looked at. You don't know how to look, you don't see, you know nothing about cinema." And he tells her, "You know nothing about tango." The distance between them is equal here, although Sally quickly tries to reach across it when she urges Pablo to join her in front of the painting *Jacob Wrestling with the Angel.* As they stand in front of it, she acknowledges the inequality of their dancing partnership by saying, "I've been following you in the tango," then pleading with him, "You have to follow me."

Pablo may hold the power, but only as long as he is the object of the look. After he and Sally perform together, he marches back to the dressing room, and they both sit facing the mirror. This shot is framed in deep focus, with Pablo in the foreground and Sally in the background. She looks from the mirror in front of her to him, but he does not flinch from his mirror image. Their argument about what went wrong with the performance degenerates into mutual accusations, at which point Sally asks him, "Where are you?" to which he replies, still looking in the mirror, "I am here." Clearly, "here" means that he is actually far from her. The next mirror scene is purely performative as Sally, having decided not to pursue her script for "Rage" and to focus on a tango film instead, returns to the two dancers who have been helping her in Buenos Aires. At night they visit the salons, and she is once again invited to dance, while Pablo looks on. She stands in their studio with the three of them, and they ask her what kind of film she intends to make; in answer, Pablo stands, pirouettes, and blows a kiss to himself in the mirror.

As they look for rehearsal space, he takes her in an elevator rather than following his friends up the stairs. The arrangement of this shot is curious, as we see her with his mirror reflection next to her. As if reacting to the extra attention Sally has been getting from his friends and other dancers, Pablo tells her that he wants to talk to her and suggests that she is not really here with him any more. Following a long and successful dance in their new rehearsal space, in which Sally seems fully in control of the three men, they return downstairs to an old barbershop. Pablo once again pulls Sally aside. Seated in a chair, looking at her from the mirror, he asks, "Are you looking at me? What do you see?" When she says that she sees him onscreen, he replies, "Then you're not here with me, you've become a camera." She replies, "But that's how I love you,

Sally becomes a mirror for Pablo and his narcissistic tendencies. © Adventure Pictures Ltd.

with my eyes." The division between mind and body, seeing and being with, is fully affirmed here. Unable to find a way to get Pablo to see her, Sally resorts to distancing herself from him. It is therefore significant that they cannot dance the tango passionately together in the same way as she dances with some of her other partners.

The Tango Lesson finally gives us male and female characters who are allowed to desire and be desired. As will be the case in *YES*, this film's protagonist is not an archetypal, spectacular woman. She is in her late forties, past the point at which women on film are typically allowed to desire. She is also not conventionally glamorous; we see her in casual clothes and with little makeup, surrounded by younger women at the salons and in an early scene in which she pitches her film to producers in Los Angeles. Although she does not fulfill the romantic-heroine stereotype, Sally's independence is evident. Further, the fact that she is recognizably "Sally Potter, real-life director" commands our attention; if we know how much she has struggled to make her past films, we would not expect to see her in a vulnerable situation or one where she is defeated. These facts also shape the way we read Sally's future actions.

There is a stark difference between Sally's black and white, bare office and the Technicolor images she conjures up for "Rage." We also notice the difference between her appearance and that of her models. She wears sensible, comfortable clothes and flat shoes—later socks—while they have impossibly high heels. She has no makeup and no accessories and is dressed for a practical purpose. The opening appearance of Sally shifts to one that is slightly more showy because of the dancing that she undertakes.

The first step toward the shift is when she has to go and buy high-heeled shoes for dancing. The scene is carefully framed to emphasize Sally's discomfort. We open with a low shot showing the floor of a corridor. Sally walks along the corridor, and although we see only her legs from calves down, it is evident from the way she is walking, pausing, and picking up her feet that she is looking down at them. After her first lesson with Gustavo and Fabián, she goes with them to the dance hall where another man approaches and asks one of the men if he can dance with her. The shoes are doing their trick, and since this pickup began with the view of the (rather old, overweight) man, Sally is constructed as an object of the gaze.

This first dance leads into an extended tango scene. As she goes from man to man, we see different kinds of tango steps, partnerships, and relationships, and the camera becomes increasingly exuberant in its movement until, by the last partner, it is simply whirling headily in circles. This captivating sequence is crucial, since it suggests that the ideal tango partnership isn't about the mind, the look, and therefore, Pablo. Instead of the uncertainty and strain that was part of her performance with Pablo, as Sally dances, her body becomes increasingly relaxed against her different partners.

Comparing this kind of dance to *Thriller,* where in arabesque the men are simply there to hold the woman up, or *The Gold Diggers,* where, waltzing, Ruby seems a mere plaything for the men, or *Orlando,* where the dances are merely a societal ritual that actually get in the way of his gaze, the couples who dance in *The Tango Lesson* share a more dynamic presence. The climax of this sequence of dancing comes with Sally's last partner, whom we see again later when he asks her to dance and is then torn away from her by Pablo.

This final partner is highly charismatic and dramatic, and he wears a strained expression across his face. The camera whirls around Sally and her partner; they both have their eyes closed, as if the pressure of the movements is simply too much for them, or as if they are joined in their reveries. They also seem to lean magically together, thereby producing single movements.

When the music finally stops, we cut to a close-up of their faces. Their noses brush as they wake from the reverie, then the man returns Sally to her teachers, remarking that it was a pleasure. The possibly licentious nature of this partner is confirmed by the behavior of the camera, which "loses itself" in head-spinning circles; the other dancers, many of whom are still watching Sally; and the hotel concierge, who greets Potter's lateness and evident all-night dancing with a curt "good morning" before he tells her how she has many, many faxes waiting. This dance comes towards the middle of the film, yet in many ways it represents a climax to Sally's attempt to tango "fifty-fifty" with a partner. The success of this partnership is conveyed by the extravagant camerawork, the people watching, and the music.

This climactic dance also helps Sally to reconcile the dancer and director parts of herself that had been in conflict in her relationship with

Sally finds a stranger with whom she can finally
dance "fifty-fifty." © Adventure Pictures Ltd.

Pablo, and which she articulated in her essay for *Projections 4* (Potter,
"Gotta"). As a tango dancer, she rediscovers her feminine side, with high
heels, flowing skirts, and a partnership where she relies on the man and
allows herself to be led. As a director, she cannot allow herself to be led.
She must remain alert and in control, an observer and commentator. In
the film she returns to Pablo for her second lesson, and there is some
harmony as their dancing extends into public spaces.

The differences between them and the failure of any coupling outside of the partnership are signaled by the books they read in the bath.
Sally reads Martin Buber's *I and Thou,* a philosophical and poetic work
about a way of being in the world with others. Buber argues that we can
either treat others as objects and make use of them for our own selfish
purposes, or we can treat them with respect and seek to understand
them as we understand ourselves. Sally's literature shows that she is
thinking about her relationship with Pablo and suggests that she has
once again adopted the critical position of observer. By contrast, Pablo
reads a biography of Marlon Brando and postures in the mirror. At

this and other moments, his reaction is superficial and even childish. However, the ideas engendered in Buber's book inform the rest of the film, as Sally seeks a union with Pablo that is free of the power play she has experienced in their dancing and yet allows each of them to feel "at home" with the other.

While several discussions of Potter's films note her skill in transforming written and spoken language and ideas using music, dance, and cinematic means, towards the end of *The Tango Lesson* we see her with the opposite aim: to put ideas into words. Thus, Sally and Pablo are partly reconciled by their joint admission of being Jewish; they visit a synagogue and talk about their partnership as a spiritual union. Given Potter's proven skill in finding ways to express the intangible, invisible, and poetic, this putting into words of a different level of union between Sally and Pablo is disappointing. Its unexpectedness in the context of the narrative also confounded many reviewers, who wanted to read from character to director and thought they had suddenly discovered that Sally Potter, the director, was admitting her Jewishness. For Ulrike Vollmer, the recourse to Jewishness can be explained as an expression of connection that is in keeping with the reference to Martin Buber's book: "Jewish identity in *The Tango Lesson* is not defined in terms of birth or belonging to a congregation but in terms of feeling related. In this sense, Sally can feel she is a Jew even without being born a Jew" (Vollmer, "'I Will Not'" 111).

In Potter's first three films, identity is explored in terms of class, nationality, and gender. *The Tango Lesson* adds the cultural/racial/religious to this list, categories to be explored more centrally in Potter's subsequent two films.

Finally Tears: *The Man Who Cried* and *YES*

The Man Who Cried

In Potter's first four films, she mixes genre and narrative conventions with experimental and avant-garde elements. In light of these films, *The Man Who Cried* emerges as Potter's most conventional and on many levels her most involving film. *The Man Who Cried* is a historical drama set in Russia, England, Paris, and the United States with an all-star cast

(Christina Ricci, Cate Blanchett, Johnny Depp, Harry Dean Stanton, and John Turturro).

In contrast to her earlier work, the style of this film is relatively unremarkable, leaving the story and characters to dominate. This is not to say that Potter has "gone mainstream" and abandoned her obsessions, themes, and interests. As a search for the father and for identity and a place to belong, *The Man Who Cried* might seem to cover new ground in Potter's oeuvre. However, once some of the key ingredients are noted—an attic in Paris; two women, one quiet and the other flirtatious; an opera company; and several men—the similarities with *Thriller* become apparent. In Suzie and Lola, Potter has reinvented Mimi and Musetta and is ready to explore what happens when they have the opportunity to be friends. The tragic tone of *Thriller*—which was enhanced by the music of *Psycho* and *La Bohème*—is in this film created by music from well-known operas and lesser-known gypsy music, and its sound track, if not the film itself, has gained much praise.

The Man Who Cried was made to appeal in a different way than Potter's other films, and despite the pleasures it provides through its strong musical strands, at times the story is ordinary and even undeveloped. Potter has said that the gypsy scenes were meant to be more extensive, but the studio made her cut over twenty scenes only days before shooting began. We should see this film as a development of key themes and a further example of Potter's exploration of nonverbal languages—camera movement and editing in *Orlando;* dance and music in *The Tango Lesson;* and music in *The Man Who Cried*—to carry emotion and affect us in more complex ways than dialogue on its own.

The observational view is assumed in this film by Fegele/Suzie (Christina Ricci), whom we first meet in her Russian home. As a little girl, Fegele is given a child's-eye view of the world, with the camera often staying at her level and therefore cutting off the heads of many of the adults. Once she moves to England and then Paris, the camera still frames her viewpoint from a low angle. For example, in Paris, where she shares a room with Lola (Cate Blanchett), Suzie is often sitting down while Lola stands, such as when they are decorating a Christmas tree or when Lola is framed from below looking up to her mirror as she does her hair, with Suzie in bed with her head at the bottom of the frame. In several sequences Suzie watches Lola and the opera singer she seduces and then is bored by, Dante (John Turturro), from the bottom of stairs looking up (as they are in her attic bedroom) or outside belowground (when they first hear Dante sing). This framing suggests that Suzie retains a childlike view of the world despite growing up; it also sets her apart from everyone except the gypsy who becomes her friend and then lover, César (Johnny Depp). Although César does not occupy a child's-eye view, he frequently lowers his eyes and therefore generally meets her gaze.

Suzie is the observer or narrator, and we often look for her reaction to events. In a bar with Dante and Lola, they talk together, but she is framed apart from them, looking on, and we constantly cut to her face as they talk. When Dante and Lola surreptitiously make love in Lola's bed, this is filmed with Suzie's face in the foreground and the couple barely in focus in the background. Even at the end of the film, on the liner as Lola talks to an old man at a table, employing her charms once more, we cut to Suzie singing and watching the flirtation.

The only time that Suzie gets to look down on someone—rather than up—is when she finally finds her father. Since he is lying in bed, she stands above him and returns to him the song he once sang for her. This framing may be a way of expressing the trauma that a child goes through if removed from his or her home and everything he or she knows. The

Like Colette and Orlando before her, Suzie is an observer/narrator. © Adventure Pictures Ltd.

child's-eye view reminds the viewer of the Russian scenes and therefore suggests that Suzie/Fegele will never be able to leave behind the past or grow away from it, even though she may no longer speak the language or have a clear memory of the people who occupied her village.

In Suzie we have a reincarnation of the troubled woman who is "lost," as we hear in *Orlando,* without a husband or father. She moves in a world populated by émigrés and those not at home, yet she is the only person who does not try to fit in. This narrative of fitting in is set in motion the moment Fegele steps off the boat. First, she is given an English name, and then she is washed and dressed in appropriate clothes. The children tease her because she will not (or cannot) speak English, then the music teacher takes her under his wing and tells her that she must fit in like he did and that he is no longer allowed to speak Welsh. He teaches her "Dido's Lament," a rather inappropriate choice by the most English of composers, Henry Purcell. In Paris she does not seek connections with people; they just seem to come to her. Lola foists herself on Suzie, then Madame Goldstein, who comments that she knows Suzie isn't like the other girls, shows her kindness once she guesses about her past. Finally, Suzie's alignment with César makes her a true outsider. From *The Tango Lesson*'s exploration of how two people might connect, the story of *The Man Who Cried* begins with the disconnection of father and daughter, which, it suggests, inflects Suzie's relationships in her inability to settle. Throughout the historical background of the suffering of the Jews and gypsies, music becomes a source of transcendence, through which one can forget the present, and grounding, through which one can remember past connections.

Suzie's inability to fit in is contrasted with Lola's chameleon-like couplings. Unlike Suzie, Lola knows exactly what she wants and how to get it. At one point she remarks that she wouldn't have gotten out of Russia without her looks, and we sense at several points that she has struggled to get to Paris. Her eagerness to share Suzie's attic room implies that despite her apparent confidence she has not found a place for herself in Paris. The key difference between Suzie and Lola is apparent in the scene in which they first hear Dante sing. Both are dressed decoratively in long satin dresses over large headdresses of feathers and wearing thick makeup (especially glossy red lipstick). They stand either side of César, who is on his horse, and gesture with their hands as fireworks are launched. Their "act" is followed by Dante's singing of "Di quelle pira" from Verdi's *Il Trovatore* (The troubadour). Appropriately, given Dante's frequent references to his family, the song is sung by a son to his mother, whom he thinks will be burnt at the stake. Ironically, it is the son who dies at the end.

Suzie and Lola are impressed by the song. In slow motion (the first of several times it is used), Suzie turns her head and looks towards the open window from which the song is audible. Lola does the same. However, the looks on their faces are completely different: Suzie is frozen, as if transported back to her father's singing, while Lola stares in fascination. Though she appears to be moved by the end of the song, Lola recomposes herself, and a look of determination crosses her face as she turns to enter the space of the party.

Throughout the song, Suzie and Lola are firmly outside of the celebrations, signaling their lower status as women who work as dancers and as visitors to Paris. They are also partly obscured from view since they have to look through the balustrade into the room; here, for once, Lola occupies Suzie's lowly position. Lola crosses over to the other side when she enters the room, leaving Suzie with César, a prophetic pairing. As she enters the room, Lola hesitates and fumbles with the back of her neck, a movement she often employs when she is lacking confidence. However, she soon sees her prey and pounces on him without further delay.

We know that Lola, like Musetta, will go from man to man. Yet at times she lets her guard down; we sense that she does want more than this, but she would never admit it. This is evident when we share time or looks with her. For example, soon after she moves in with Dante, we see her luxuriating in a foam bath, yet she seems incredibly bored. Or later, taking a taxi after a party with the Germans, during which Dante reveals to the commandant that Suzie is Jewish, Lola looks nervous. Or even when she and Suzie succeed in getting on the boat to New York, she tries to justify to Suzie her relationship with the new man. These moments of candor are balanced by Suzie's unspoken comments on her behavior, which we are party to through the many reaction shots from her.

Suzie generally assumes the same alienated expression with Lola as she did with her foster mother. Soon after arriving in England and being delivered to her foster family, Suzie is scrubbed in the bath by her foster mother, then she sits on her new bed in a warm nightdress. In both scenes, her expression suggests distance and observation, and this expression is repeated with Lola. Yet Suzie has much to thank Lola for. While we assume that Suzie found herself her apartment, Lola keeps bringing her on extra jobs and ensures Suzie a safe departure from Paris despite her guilt over Dante's betrayal of her.

Seeing Lola as a Musetta character, a good-time girl who nevertheless tries to befriend Suzie/Mimi, casts her as the seducing woman who cannot seem to move out of the position of object, with the slight power over men that it offers. We know nothing of Lola's family (apart from the fact that they were poor) because she has few loyalties. Her "roots" mean little to her; indeed, they are what she is fleeing from.

A very different attitude to displacement is taken by Dante, whose bluster and pride in his traumatic upbringing suggests a closeness to his proletarian roots. However, his arrogance onstage and complete disregard for anyone but himself undercuts this. In front of the commandant, we see his terror that he might be tarred with the same brush as Perlman; he betrays Suzie shortly after, as if to prove which side he is on. His Italian pride is nationalistic in flavor; hence he is prejudiced against Jews and gypsies.

Dante complies with Lola's seduction, but it is easy to see another side to him, where he wants more than Lola can give. Later in the film, as he tries to kiss Suzie, he praises the way that they have struggled to get where they are. The implication seems to be that Lola didn't have to struggle and that he despises her for this. Dante is probably the most contradictory character in the film. He sings his songs with much passion and—we assume from people's reactions—much talent, and there is a side to him that is sensitive and allied with the lovers or tragic heroes in the operas in which he stars. However, he courts Lola for sex, is arrogant and rude to everyone around him, and supports Italian fascism. These contradictions come to a head when he flees to a church as France is occupied and curls up like a baby on the pew—before singing for the Germans.

With the characters of Suzie, Lola, and Dante, Potter explores the effects of exile and identity on one's behavior and aspirations; yet she puts a new tint on these issues with the inclusion of the gypsies and most importantly César, played by the heartthrob Johnny Depp. Suzie's first encounter with gypsies comes as a little girl, when she is playing with her father in the forest. The moving camera and swish pans create an innocent, idealistic picture of the relationship between father and daughter as one hides from the other. This tone shifts as first we hear a loud sound of flapping wings, though we don't see a bird, and then we see the daughter running away, oblivious to the fact that her father has stopped running and is anxiously calling her name. We see the girl hiding from him behind a tree. As she peeks out, she sees a caravan of gypsy travelers. This first entrance of the gypsies shifts the mood of ease with her environment and foreshadows the departure of Suzie's father soon after this scene. The gypsies are invading sources of strangeness that Suzie does not really comprehend.

The second time Suzie encounters gypsies, they represent her left-behind past, something more familiar than her new life in England, where she cannot yet speak the language. We encounter Suzie being bullied in the playground. "Where are you from?" the children ask but don't wait for an answer. We cut to the sound of smashing glass, and her foster mother comes downstairs to see Suzie smashing all of the woman's family photos. She slaps her. We return to the playground, where Suzie encounters the same behavior as before. The camera pans around her, and in the time it takes to make this movement, Suzie has walked away from the children towards the entrance gate, where a crowd is gathering and chanting, "Gypsies!" The ringing of the school bell forces most children to run away, but Suzie stays by the gate, and we see caravans. This scene is shot in a similar manner to the first encounter, with Suzie hiding behind the bars, separated from the gypsies. However, this time they seem to spark something in her, representing her lost home, and she begins to sing to them.

These connections between Suzie and the gypsies prepare us for her main relationship with César. The possibility of a connection between them is immediately raised the first time they are together. Suzie, who is turning away to take off her ridiculous headdress, is immediately captivated. She turns back towards the song in slow motion. César observes Suzie's haunted look from high on his horse and leans down and puts his hand on her shoulder. She looks up at him, still not really with it, then watches him as he gallops off. This first encounter is a complex moment. Suzie is transported by Dante's singing, and because of the way that music has been used to represent her past up to now, we assume that she is once again thinking of what she has lost. César's presence underlines this, since as a gypsy he may also remind her of that lost time. However, her reaction to his hand on her shoulder suggests that she does not see him as part of her reveries; indeed, Dante's singing has more of a place there than the awkward, uncomprehending César.

This initial encounter also lacks something romantically. If we compare it to the initial scene between Orlando and Shelmerdine, romance and a sense of connection is absent between Suzie and César. Shortly after finding themselves facing each other on the turf, both in vulnerable positions, Orlando and Shelmerdine decide that they feel as one, as if each knows everything about the other (who is no longer other). By contrast, the eventual relationship between Suzie and César retains a sense of their difference from each other. Though both are outsiders to Dante and his world and both have no roots, César insists that he has his family with him, and he knows who he is. Time is spent at César's gypsy hangouts, dancing and drinking or, when Suzie ends up at their camp, singing.

The attraction between César and Suzie is ambivalent. He taunts her, racing away on his horse while she rides her bike, and calls her "degagi" and further provokes, "Then what are you?" Yet when he sees her with others, dancing in the café with Pablo Veron or singing in the camp for the other men, he appears to look on approvingly and with desire. In the seduction scene, César gallops around Suzie in slow motion, in true romantic-hero fashion. Yet once he lies on top of her, she is unsure. The next scene shows Suzie splashing water on her face as Orlando does following her transformation from male to female and SHE does just before welcoming HE back in YES. The contrast between the fire that was the backdrop to their lovemaking and this water might suggest a rebirth for Suzie. Yet the fact that it remains her secret while Lola chatters away about "no more boring money problems" suggests that Suzie is not sure about the relationship or where it will go; therefore it may not be as life-changing as, visually, it appears.

Given the lack of successful couplings in Potter's films, the strangeness of the Suzie/César pairing is not out of character. Since César is a complete outsider, he underlines Suzie's decision to remain on the outside rather than fitting in, as her Welsh singing teacher has asserted she must do. He is even more of an outsider than she is. However, because to a certain extent César is complete—he has a family and a purpose in life—Suzie is forced to keep traveling and looking for her father.

As Potter has pointed out, a "cry" can be a song as well as a sound associated with tears, and the title of the film evokes the first man who cries in Potter's work: Rodolpho. Overcome with grief, throwing himself on her bed, the hero of *La Bohème* sings "Mimi" as the strings rise and the chords thunder. Yet *Thriller*'s feminist investigation of this story suggests that Rodolpho's cry, however heartfelt, is ultimately self-centered and at the expense of Mimi. By contrast, in *The Man Who Cried,* the father whose cry opens the film, Dante whose cries provide the sound track for the events, and César who sheds tears while Suzie sleeps before they part are far more well-rounded and complex characters.

While Rodolpho's cry is unheard by Mimi, the men in this film have a great effect on Suzie, shaping her life and energizing her living. The title also cues us in to the importance of the men, and like Pablo, Dante and César are allowed a complexity and understanding that was never present in Potter's earlier films, in which the men are to be blamed and therefore appear stereotyped and one-dimensional. All of which prepares us for *YES*, where we have a male character who is intelligent and thoughtful, attractive and appealing, as important as the female, and who begins a relationship that seems open, genuine, and giving.

YES

After the big-budget mainstream experience of *The Man Who Cried*, it is not surprising that Potter turned to a low-budget project over which she had greater control and was more able to experiment. Potter has described *YES* as a reaction to September 11, 2001. She decided to address the increasing divisions between the West and the Middle East through a love story involving the meeting of both worlds that ends in Cuba, an idealized space closed off from capitalist conflicts.

The central couple in *YES*, known only as "SHE" (Joan Allen) and "HE" (Simon Abkarian), visually resemble Sally and Pablo in *The Tango Lesson.* Sally's closing song to Pablo therefore seems apt: "You are me and I am you, / One is one and one are two." The problem posed in *The Tango Lesson*—how to come together while respecting differences—is echoed in *YES*. The union of bodies and equal giving from both sides is the challenge of the tango, in which each partner must give to the other. The woman must not resist the man's lead, while the man must not force the woman. This ideal is seen metaphorically in *YES*, in which we can compare the role of each tango partner to what HE and SHE have to achieve to be together.

The message of *YES* has been growing throughout Potter's career: differences must be put aside, and connections must be made with people rather than positions, an essence rather than an appearance. However, in this film the couple's conflict is played out around issues of race and religion that were first mooted in *The Tango Lesson*. As usual in Potter's films, there are many obstructions to connection—first, from the characters themselves and the people and social and cultural pressures around them; and second, from the film's style, which cuts against romance and reminds us that there is always more than one way to see anything.

The titular *YES* can be read in many different ways. It could suggest a coming together that is all-encompassing and embraced equally by both sides. In the context of Potter's career, *YES* also represents the ultimate movement away from the cinema of antipleasure in which narrative, spectacle, and illusionism were denied with a resounding "NO." *YES* uses many of Potter's distancing techniques, and she still can't bring herself to make a romantic movie. However, there is more room for connections between characters and audience. The telling of the tale transforms it, but in *YES* the iambic pentameter in which the dialogue is written adds a poetic layer to sound and image that reminds one of the richness of meaning first encountered in *The Gold Diggers*. The dialogue shifts from the straightforward, as SHE describes to her scientist colleagues what she is being asked to do,

> SHE: I understand that you've invited me
> To make a case that life begins at three
> Hours; or at one, or two, or maybe four,
> As if there is a moment when we can be sure
> That we are human, (Potter, *YES* 8)

to the "litany" of her dead aunt,

> If and when I die
> I want to see you cry

I want to see you tear your hair
Your howls of anguish fill the air
I want to see you beat your breast
And rent your clothes and all the rest
And, sobbing, fall upon my bed . . .
I want to know that I am dead, (61)

to the use of words to seduce,

SHE: Speak to me.
HE: Of what? What is there to say?
SHE: Too much . . . or nothing . . . please try, anyway.
[He thinks for a moment, and then:]
HE: Well, I adore . . . the number one.
One you, one me, one moon, one sun.
SHE: Must I revolve around you then? Am I
The silver planet circling the gold?
Are you the source of light and heat, whilst I
Am shadow, pulling watery tides, and cold? (14)

The delivery of this verse reminds us of the dual roles of actor and performer that Potter used to cast her films. The actors in YES are given rhymes that were written to convey their regional accents (as in the kitchen hands who work with HE), their moods (the clipped, metaphorical language HE and SHE use as they confront each other in an underground parking lot), and even their generational differences (Grace, the goddaughter of SHE whose replies are often matter-of-fact and curt). The actors perform this language and act their roles; in so doing, they allow us to extract the verse from the people and apply its deferral of meaning across the whole of the film.

YES picks up the difficulty of coming together into two that is present in *The Tango Lesson* and *The Man Who Cried.* However, while the narrative of the film explores this difficulty, on another level, the verse, and particularly the dialogue between HE and SHE, treats the wider theme of the confrontation between Christianity and Islam, figured through a privileged white female and an exiled man from the Middle East. Imagery of light and dark, water and fire are used throughout to depict the meeting of cultures, religions, ideologies, and individuals.

The seduction and courtship takes place first in his apartment, then later in a restaurant. In the first scene, the pattern of imagery is established by him describing them as "one moon, one sun"; her reply leads to his protracted response. The scene finishes with him saying, "No, lovely lady. All I meant to say / Was this: you are the one. The light of day, / The velvet night, the single rose, the hand / I want to hold" (Potter, *YES* 16).

Such imagery develops in several ways. In the scene that follows, HE is working in his kitchen with other kitchen hands. We join them mid-conversation, and they are discussing women, particularly blonde, white women. The juxtaposition of these two scenes suggests the way that race inflects the descriptions chosen by HE, each of which revolves around the characteristics of whiteness: blonde, golden, and the light of the world. As if to pun on this, the black Caribbean, Virgil, chooses these words to express how he's "had it" with blondes: "I've seen the light." Then he says that he's turned away from temptation to God. Significantly, although HE does not seem to be overly attentive to this conversation, HE also will reject SHE as a kind of temptress Eve figure.

The symbolism continues in an amorous encounter in a restaurant. HE tells her, "[Y]ou light the lamp / That guides me through the velvet night / Towards you." Then he changes his metaphors: "Your hungry look ignites my fire. / Oh lady, what then can I do / But burn? I am in flames for you." Her response describes a similar sense of heat: "[Y]ou hold me and I melt" (Potter, *YES* 30). In their final encounter, when HE tries to break it off, SHE tells him, "My mind's on fire" (51). The elemental images of water and fire describe passion and the couple's effect on each other. Yet at the same time, the danger and dark underside of those passions, how they might be seen in light of the responsibility of these two people, are also part of this imagery. When HE decides to break it off, it is because of her whiteness, her goldenness, and because, he says, "Your country is a dragon breathing flames" (53), referring to the wars between East and West.

This elemental imagery might also remind us of *The Gold Diggers*, in which some of the philosophies of the alchemists are embedded in the film, with its hint at the "celestial ruby." The affair between HE and SHE, at its most intimate, seems to be an alchemical mix of the magical and the dangerous. If we add to this the fact that SHE is a scientist, looking for the "secret" moment when life begins, and what drives her to hold on to HE is the death of her aunt and thus the reminder of her own mortality, the scene is set for Potter's familiar contemplation of mortality (*Orlando*), destiny, and choice (*The Man Who Cried* and *The Tango Lesson*).

While the central couple do connect, many of the other characters remain isolated from each other. This isolation is expressed first in the way in which we are party to characters' thoughts and therefore know things that others do not. We hear SHE thinking about Anthony and HE, and Anthony thinking about SHE; we also hear the dying aunt's final thoughts. The knowledge we have as a result of this system of confidences isolates the characters, since we know how they deceive each other. We are cued in to this system by the cleaner's opening monologue, which tells how she sees and therefore knows everything:

> I doubt
> They'll ever realize I know it all.
> They think that those of us who clean are small
> Somehow, in body and mind; we fall
> Out of their line of sight; invisible.

The cleaner's point of view is continued through the film as we return to her for further monologues and are also treated to other looks to camera by those cleaning and sweeping.

The cleaner's speech prepares us for the film's prying into the private life of SHE and our access to people's thoughts. She also sets up a reversal of customary oppositions, such as inside and outside and large and small, all of which could be seen as a "cleaner's-eye view" of reality, a view that connects the hidden, such as dust and dirt, with what is hidden from others, such as characters' thoughts. From this point on, we will be party to the whispered thoughts of SHE and Anthony and moments of subjectivity indicated by the overemphasized sound track. This begins as SHE returns from the bathroom at dinner, and we hear what HE said to her when they first met. The first time he phones her, when she is in the United States, the sound is strange, with a skateboarder outside her cab overwhelming their conversation. At home, Anthony and SHE dine together but fall out almost as soon as they sit down. HE stands with his back to her, staring into the mirror

We are introduced to the cleaner's-eye view of reality. © Nicola Dove, Eye Box.

and contemplating—in his head and on the sound track—how on earth their relationship fell apart like this.

Potter's refusal to name the couple suggests a certain generalization, while the thoughts we share with the cleaner and SHE cut against this, suggesting intimacy. These paradoxical relations are carried through by the camera movement and mise-en-scène. Framing and focus frequently emphasize relations between foreground and background that we might otherwise miss; and lighting and the grain of the image underline foreground and background and the switches and distortions of perspective that can be achieved by looking differently. The film opens with bauble-like circles in the air that we realize are dust particles thrown up by cleaner's vacuum cleaning and shaking of the duvet. These particles linger in the air, where they are enlarged and slowed down so that they dominate our view. The shot is reminiscent of the crucial sex-change scene in *Orlando* and its profusion of glowing particles, lit by the sunlight as Orlando washes her face. In both films, these shots enlarge the invisible, showing us what we would typically ignore or be unaware of. They suggest that what will follow will be a different perspective than what we have been used to.

In *YES*, these dust particles are followed by a series of distortions of space and time. First we get grainy, overlit images and slowed-down footage of SHE in a taxi with Anthony, then a time-lapse black-and-white view through the surveillance camera at the restaurant when SHE and Anthony enter, or later when SHE hands her card to HE for further contact. In these examples, what is normally unseen is revealed, or that which we might have seen and then dismissed remains onscreen for longer.

Perspective is played around with in a number of ways. Several shots use high, low, or expressionistic angles so that the relationship between body and space is distorted, and bodies assume unreal proportions, being either Lilliputian or gigantic. The camera movements also contribute to these distortions. As with Potter's previous films, the camera is rarely still. For example, the kitchen scenes are filmed with a handheld camera and swish pans, which enables the disparate characters to be separate in space yet connected in time such that their varied points of view can be fully appreciated. Or later, as SHE lies in bed watching HE prepare food in his kitchen, the camera pans and tilts to keep him in frame, giving the scene a restlessness instead of calm. This feeling increases as she replies that she does know how he feels about his "holy war," and she expresses this in voiceover as the image is slowed down and the camera tilts horizontally.

The most consistent play with perspective comes through the startling framing, as foreground and background constantly interfere with each other. Our impression of what is important is confused, and we see objects or parts of spaces as we have never seen them before, as if in a bid to instate the cleaner's view that "everything is connected" and it's really all about your point of view.

There are many examples of this. The first occurs at the husband's dinner party. Following their arrival at the grand building, filmed on the surveillance camera, we see the husband greeted by a crowd of people, while the wife wanders into the dining room alone and is framed in a long shot such that SHE is almost drowning in the space. This is how HE finds her for the first time. After matching shots in which we see the back of her head as she turns away from us, we swiftly cut to the back of his head as he rushes through the kitchen and out into the dining area. He walks past her, then turns and walks back towards her. Asking if SHE is alright, HE proceeds to talk seductively.

We do not hear most of his words until later, when SHE is in the bathroom recalling them. At this stage, his words are cut off by an edit showing her sitting rigidly at the table, surrounded by people. Although those around her talk to others and are generally animated, SHE is the only person fully in focus, still and upright and differentiated from the other guests. Her husband sits to her right on the far side of the large table. We cut across the table with the focus adjusting slightly every time, but SHE and her husband are constantly framed with other people in the way. While the people who get in the way of the wife's view of the husband are all women, therefore fueling her distress at his infidelity, those surrounding SHE seem oblivious to her. As SHE becomes increasingly isolated by the framing, HE makes a connection with her through eye contact and then teasing expressions that make her laugh through her tears.

We next encounter this shift in perspective during her talk in the United States. SHE stands at the far end of a long, highly polished oval table; people are seated on either side, watching her, and they have tall glasses of water in front of them. She outlines the project they have set her: to define the moment of life. Then she switches—"but wait a minute"—and the camera angle changes to the left-hand side so that we look at her through several of the glasses. Perspective is distorted by these now large glasses, and she appears like a giantess, while the people on the left seem small. She says, "[C]ould objectivity be just a point of view?" We cut once more to the other side of the table, and an out-of-focus glass now fills half the frame with SHE just about visible behind it.

The focus is pulled slightly and distorted as SHE talks of those scientists who thought they could see a "little man inside" the sperm. These stylistic distortions are obviously in keeping with the subject of her talk, but they could equally be seen as continuations of the cleaner's-eye view or even an indication of her state of mind, having uncovered her husband's infidelity and been approached by another man shortly after.

Trees rather than glasses serve as our enlarged objects in the next scene of distortions. HE has called her to walk and eat. We begin with a tracking shot looking up at a sky filled with trees in blossom. We dissolve to behind a tree that fills half the frame, to the left of which the lovers walk. We dissolve to behind them as they walk along the path, then dissolve once more to behind the tree. This time the camera pans left so that it can see them, then pans back behind the tree, framing them with one of its large branches curving on top of them.

The blossom and the spring day suggest this as an idealized image, but the camera is shy of this interpretation and instead awkwardly bobs back and forth, always framing them in relation to the trees, whose giant trunks and branches show their age. While the couple talk of where they have come from, the passing of time is emphasized such that, though their impending coupling is central to the film, it is relativized in the scheme of things: blossoms will grow and the seasons will change without them. As if to underline that their story is a small part of a wider picture, the final shot of them walking, now from in front of them but still panning from behind the trees, also captures a group of women wearing chador and walking behind them. It is over this image that she talks of religion and her Catholic upbringing.

The final scene in which distortion is used is again in a restaurant where the lovers are together. We dissolve very slowly from SHE walking out of her laboratory to the restaurant, the camera panning from the window to the inside. The opening of the image previews the techniques that will be used as we are given the view through the window outside the restaurant, reflections on this window, and what remains of the scene before. As the pan continues, however, the screen clears, and we are left looking wholly at the couple.

We dissolve to a closer shot framing them from waist to head and with a wine glass just perceptible in the foreground left. The camera continues tracking left, and the glass moves out of frame but is replaced by another one. We dissolve to an even closer shot that was filmed at six frames per second and then stretched to twenty-four to give the impression of slow motion, and the camera begins to bob up and down, framing them through one glass and then another. As we pass these reflective objects, images are reflected and distorted. SHE appears smaller in the glass, then blurred as the camera passes it. The impression of slow motion continues until a waiter comes over with a menu. We return to the camera's bobbing and the slow motion, and the camera peers over and then through the glasses once more.

Like the use of mirrors in *The Tango Lesson* and the problematization of the male gaze in *Orlando,* this camera movement is designed to make seeing difficult. On the one hand, when SHE is talking to the table of listeners in the United States, the framing through glasses underlines the theme of her talk: that the moment of genesis of a life is a matter of point of view. On the other hand, in those scenes with the couple in the park or the restaurant, there seems to be a will to represent what might be seen as common seduction scenes differently.

As the couple walk under the blossoming trees surrounded by spring daffodils, the scene appears endlessly romantic. But the camera will not allow such a simple interpretation. Instead, its antics—moving side to side while the couple moves vertically away from the camera—is distracting. With the repetitive music of Philip Glass, this scene reads as emblematic of the film's theme of the minute details and the global picture. On the minute level, we have the couple, their specificities—which is what they talk about in this scene—and their genuine feelings.

On the global level, we have what they stand for—another way of reading this dialogue—and the misunderstandings that arise when we relate to them only on this level. This is the substance of the argument in the parking lot: HE has let SHE become a stand-in for a Western ideal, an opposition that he feels he should abhor. The scene in the restaurant acts as the climax of their stages of intimacy, as they are able to relate to one another on an erotic level and in public. The camera movement adds to the seduction of SHE by HE, since it suspends the action and gets in the way while suggesting, like the camera that hides behind the trees, the illicit nature of their affair. The camera spies, suggesting a third person looking at the couple, and participates in the seductions, delaying the climax, stirring unease, and creating complex images.

Once we add to these seduction scenes the use of footage from the surveillance camera in his restaurant and kitchen, further themes emerge around who looks at whom and how they do so. The surveillance camera is used as a kind of Big Brother control mechanism, through which the restaurant boss (the familiar George Yiasoumi) can keep an eye on his kitchen, as well as a more poetic, often overlooked view in which we see the distance between SHE and her husband as they enter the dinner, or as she gives him her card despite having just asserted in the bathroom that she must "say no" to his advances.

Like the use of choreography in *Thriller* or the songs in *The Gold Diggers,* these images offer a nonverbal level of communication. The couple's first encounter is one of the most powerful in any Potter film, equal to Sally's first view of Pablo in *The Tango Lesson*. First we have the parallel editing of their backs, which matches them as HE enters the dining room in a Steadicam shot and walks efficiently towards the table, passing her on his way. He stops abruptly, having glanced towards her as he moves past, then turns back and approaches her. At this point her back is towards us, so we still look at the back of her neck. This is our first encounter with HIM, and SHE is unaware of his look; however, his desire or sensitivity towards her is evident in a way that we have not seen before in Potter's films.

As viewers, we have been privy to her hurt, and HE also seems to feel it. Although we do not hear the full impact of what he says to her, the moment when SHE replays it in the bathroom, she once again stands with her back to us, and we can therefore imagine his gaze at her back and him saying those words. From the beginning of the film, his desiring, attentive gaze is evident and is opposed with the lack of attention paid to her by her husband. Any suggestion that his gaze or desire might overpower her is allayed in the love scenes, in which they are filmed equally and their dialogue plays out the complexities of coupling.

YES makes use of slow dissolves, and the effect is such that everything appears to be connected, and time and space play over one another, as if we can simply dive from one image into another. We are persuaded to see the relationship between the micro and the macro through dissolves such as that from the organisms that SHE looks at through her microscope to a high-angled matching shot of the kitchen HE works in, with its similar matching dots and squiggles of men at work. The self-consciousness that these dissolves, the moving camera, and at times the poetic dialogue bring to the drama are emphasized further in the moment when the various female cleaners look at the camera.

In addition to the cleaner/observer figure at home, we have sweepers in her laboratory and at the swimming pool and at one point the kitchen staff, all of whom pass the camera slowly and, at a crucial moment, look up at us with expressionless faces. This sense of connection, and of details relating to a wider picture, is picked up through the breadth of the characters. We meet women of all ages, from the teenage Grace, obsessed with her body's imperfections, to Grace's mother, friend of

SHE and ultimately the lover of Anthony, to the cleaner and the dying aunt. The very different options open to women are represented by these characters, as we see women working for other women, as career women, as mothers, and those, such as the aunt, who have taken a more political stance in life. Although each character represents a different position, each is fleshed out, as is evident at the end of the film when we encounter each once more.

For the men, there are a similar array of positions, with the kitchen staff, HE, and the husband. The husband is rarely seen outside the house, thus associating him, rather than the wife, with domestic spaces. SHE is rarely at home; instead, we largely see her at work and with HE. It is also evident that for Anthony this house is his private space, as we catch him more than once playing air guitar to his Eric Clapton music, filmed from a low angle to suggest his entrapment. When Grace unwittingly visits him, looking for her godmother, his inappropriate intimacy also suggests that he is lonely. Grace's retelling of the husband's confidences to SHE betrays his candor and indicates the younger generation's misunderstanding of the old.

YES repeats many of *Orlando's* successful strategies by embedding a strong narrative within an experimental structure. However, *YES* goes further, complicating this combination through poetic dialogue and the underlying political theme of East meeting West. The politics temper the romance, and the poetry strengthens the symbolism that has been opened up by the cleaner's-eye view. The effect of all of these layers of meaning is aptly summarized by the closing image, invoked at the beginning of this book. HE and SHE are on a beach in Cuba; they embrace and kiss. The meeting of their mouths is slowed down so that they become smeared lines of flight. But the film does not end here. Instead, we gradually dissolve so that we begin to see inside these faces a dividing cell, which develops and is exchanged across the mouths of the two. Once again, what could have been a romantic climax is undercut. The dissolve reminds us that the characters have merely been a tool through which Potter, or the cleaner, has explored how a couple might overcome appearances and respond to an essential self. Appearance is reduced to essence in this shot, and then this is also wiped away as we dissolve once more to waves upon the shore and the word "YES."

Endings

If we return to the closing images of *YES*, we might attempt a consideration of how closure works for films that are intent on asking questions and a director who always has more to say. In Potter's early films, with their rejection of linear narrative and instatement instead of collage and musical themes as structuring presences, it is obvious that closure was not an option. *Thriller* and *The Gold Diggers* end with affirmations of stories that are only beginning. Mimi's "maybe we could have loved one another"—the admission of a missing relationship—propels Potter's subsequent narratives. Like Virginia Woolf's discovery that female characters rarely get to be friends or companions in novels, this ending sets up a space of absence to be filled, a call for future female alliances. Celeste's "even as I look and even as I see I am changing what is there" emphasizes that Potter will keep looking and changing. Both films are critical in the sense that they act out a dissatisfaction with how cinema has transcribed the place of the female. However, neither really knows how to allow desire, pleasure, the gaze, and the voice that it has insisted is missing.

Influenced by Potter's performance art as well as the context of deconstruction in the late 1970s and early 1980s, these early films seem content to juxtapose and deny rather than trying to be constructive. These films are unsatisfying, yet they fit within their deconstructive critical context as examples of the first stage of engagement with the problems of cinematic pleasure for women. One reason for the "taking apart" of Potter's first two films has to do with the primal stage of her style, which would not develop fully until *Orlando*. This film's ending, tying in with that of the book and yet extending it into the contemporary moment, suggests a progression: instead of Mimi's voice from the grave that can't go anywhere, or the women-only fantasy space in which Celeste and Ruby swim, we have the future promise posed by Orlando's daughter, and the importance of the gaze is affirmed by the daughter's wielding of the video camera. Orlando's pronouncement through the voiceover that she has let go of the past could serve as a metaphor for Potter's own practice. *Orlando* should be seen as a new beginning, with Potter moving forward in a positive direction and expanding on themes built up so far. The fantasy and performance that characterize her first two films is not fully rejected but is present in the figure of the angel.

The song, dance, and kiss that close *The Tango Lesson* suggest that a healing process might be going on. Finally Pablo opens and confesses his fallibility, and Sally eases this by suggesting how a relationship between them might be possible. The fact that this is suggested as something that will counteract Pablo's fear of "disappearance without a trace" itself implies a moving forward. However, this scene takes place in a space we have not seen before. The setting appears to be a port, with massive cranes that tower over the couple as they dance. Given the nocturnal setting, with pools of light into which the couple dance, it is as if we have returned to the performance space familiar from *Thriller* and *The Gold Diggers*. Differences have not necessarily been resolved, and the romantic union is far from sealed; nevertheless, a point of understanding has been reached.

Suzie's singing to her father in *The Man Who Cried* is probably the strongest sort of closure in any of Potter's films. Suzie's quest for her identity or roots—or, more simply, for her father, someone who shares her past—is at an end. We do not know what will happen to her or how long her father will last beyond this meeting, and his new family is an obvious point of unease. But her quest has an end point, and her voice has returned. The fact that she chooses to sing to him rather than talk reiterates the theme of the power of song for invoking memory, emotion, and a bond that goes beyond the verbal. We experience this transformative power the first time Suzie hears Dante sing. In contrast to Potter's other films, the conclusion of *The Man Who Cried* takes us backwards rather than forwards in the sense that the reunion with her father represents the end to her quest. She has found the only person who can verify her origins and with whom she does not have to fit in but can be herself.

Finally, in *YES*, the cleaner's monologue rhymes the beginning and ending of the film, confirming that it has been an exploration of how "when you look closer, nothing goes away." Potter's insistence that we "look closer" is only the latest of a series of different looks that her films have tried on and worked through. Her insistence on looking differently and looking again has kept her making films. For Potter, there is always more to be done, said, seen, desired, and thought.

An Interview with Sally Potter

August 18, 2004

CATHERINE FOWLER: It's apparent from previous interviews that you decided pretty early on that you wanted to be a filmmaker, so I wonder if you could talk about the environment you were raised in that might have brought about that desire.

SALLY POTTER: Interestingly enough, I've just been having discussions with two close friends from very different backgrounds: one an Indian man, a writer, who came from a Hindu background, and another actress friend who came from a Christian background. I found myself talking about the fact that I came from an atheist and an anarchist background, which meant that, unlike them, I grew up in an environment that was full of questions, where nothing could be taken for granted. Everything had to be worked out from scratch. There was no holding belief system in which there were any givens whatsoever. And I think that whilst that creates a feeling of perpetual cultural exile, for you are, in effect, an outsider in your own culture, it also gives the advantage of years of practice of at least the attempt of independent thought. It was quite a poor background, materially, but I would say rich in ideas and with the constant presence of music.

CF: So quite a liberating background as well.

SP: Liberating in some ways, not liberating in other ways, because I think that any background like that is, in fact, full of contradictions. And a liberal background is also one where the boundaries are confused, because there are really no limits. Therefore I grew up in a context of extreme freedom that can also produce anxiety and emotional confusion. But it was intellectually liberating, yes.

CF: Equally, you started at a place in the filmmaking world that I suppose was on the margins, wasn't it?

SP: It was on the margins, and I was on the margins, but one should never underestimate the material conditions that produce an aesthetic, and I was a penniless student with a camera trying to figure out what I could do with nothing. Nothing's changed, actually; the same principle seems to apply now! *Jerk,* for example, was a simple exploration of what twenty-four frames a second means and what happens if you treat every single frame as if it is a different frame rather than part of the illusion of flow. Now very fast images like that have become familiar, but they weren't familiar at the time. Looked at in another way, I was spinning out my one little reel of film and making it last as long as possible by giving each frame a value. And of course, it was the early days of what was then called underground filmmaking in the U.K., where the language of film itself was under scrutiny, and nothing could be taken for granted.

CF: Were you aware of all that?

SP: The underground film movement defined itself against America, or at least, against the values of Hollywood. But it was an ambivalent, love/hate relationship, certainly in my case, because I adored American musicals, loved the Marx brothers, loved a great deal of American cinema and literature, as well as individual Americans. But I was certainly anti-American imperialism, including the "imperialism of the imagination." I asked myself repeatedly: What does it mean to be a fourteen-year-old, twenty-year-old, or thirty-year-old in England making cinema, with a camera but almost no money? How does that relate to the cinema made with millions of dollars as part of a huge global industry in America? Is it even the same form? Can they both be called cinema just because a camera is involved? And I felt that I was part of the same form but in a state of argument with it, debate perhaps.

CF: So it had to be there so you could argue with that.

SP: It simply was there—and very powerfully—so one could agree with it, or argue with it. But equally Godard was there, and the work of Eisenstein, so all was one in a sense. All was part of the history of cinema, which I learned from, measured myself against, tried to find my way through.

CF: You have already mentioned some other directors, but what were your cultural influences in those early days?

SP: My influences were extremely eclectic: from Chekhov to Billie Holiday, from Eisenstein to the Ealing comedies. Godard, Buñuel, Fellini, Bergman, Tarkovsky, Orson Welles, Powell/Pressburger . . . work by the great masters that I watched again and again . . . these were my teachers, in addition to the lesser known avant-gardists. I learned by doing and by watching, by dancing and by singing, by reading and by editing. *Singing in the Rain* was a better teacher for me about the "signs" of cinema than Levi-Strauss or any of the structuralists. Struggling with *Thriller*, alone, through long dark nights in the Filmmakers' Co-op editing rooms; putting together and pulling apart strips of film—the mistakes I made taught me more than any theories about montage. Moving in the bright lights onstage taught me more about the vulnerability and omnipotence of the performer working with the energy of the eyes of the audience than any theories of "the gaze." Politically speaking, I wanted to think internationally, to see myself as part of a global history of the making of things.

CF: Thinking about the other things that were going on when you made your first film, your performing, dancing, composing, and singing, did you ever think at any stage that you were going to go down one of those paths? Or when film came along, was that it?

SP: I was in a state of gross confusion, crisis in fact, for a long time about choices, about which and what to do. Terrified that I would become a sort of Jack . . . Jacklyn of all trades, mistress of none. But my first, really passionate commitment to a form—after writing, which came earlier—was to filmmaking. I announced to the world at fourteen that I was going to be a film director and was totally laughed down, but that was my chosen path. My meandering route through dance, which was also therapeutic, interesting, and a social activity, compared to the solitary filmmaking of the kind that I was doing, led to live work, to theater, and a primary relationship with an audience.

The discipline of improvisation, in music and in performance, has influenced everything I do. The continuous attempt to be "in the present," reacting to and in dialogue with what is there, is a large part of my process at every stage of making a film. In my twenties I must have played/sung/performed in hundreds of events/concerts/festivals around Europe . . . many of them New Music/jazz-based events (with Limited Dance Company, FIG [Feminist Improvisation Group], the Film Music Orchestra, solo shows, et cetera), all based on improvisation as an art form. In effect, it is the ultimate form of influence by one's peers—a kind of "deep listening."

As well as these influences, music had always been a part of my life, and gradually the strands kind of knitted together. I returned to film whenever I had the money. I eventually made a decision in my late twenties with *Thriller* that if I hadn't made a film by the age of thirty that I was proud of and that somehow broke out of this kind of spider's web–like ghetto of invisibility that I felt I was in, I would change tack completely in my life. But *Thriller* did break out, and that encouraged me to go on.

CF: Sticking with the context of your early films, were you aware of other feminist work at the time?

SP: I never saw *Jeanne Dielman* [*Jeanne Dielman 23 quai du commerce Bruxelles;* dir. Chantal Akerman; Belgium, 1975] and still haven't, but I was aware of its aura. I did see *Riddles of the Sphinx* [dir. Laura Mulvey and Peter Wollen; U.K., 1976]. I knew Laura and Peter already: they used to come to my live events and performances. But we didn't come from the same background. Chantal Akerman was very much part of European filmmaking—a movement of independence that was on a slightly more popular level I would say, than its equivalent in Britain. Laura Mulvey and Peter Wollen came from an academic background and a theoretical one and approached film from that perspective.

As for the feminist tag—a word which I rarely use about my work anymore, but people still use about it all the time—the feminist movement, and its literature in particular, was hugely influential for me as a body of ideas about female experience and as an explanation for why I and my friends felt the way we did about ourselves and our place in the world—the politics of relationships. It was a worldview that changed my life. The personal *was* political. I went to conferences and talked with friends avidly and was a member of some "consciousness-raising" groups, so I guess I was part of the loose conglomeration called the women's movement, which in fact, at the time, just seemed very ad hoc. And again because I wasn't part of the academic world, I wasn't part of the strand of more organised feminist rhetoric.

But where I differed very strongly from some women who called themselves feminist artists was that I thought to call one's work anything-ist was a massive mistake, just like social-realist, Stalinist, or whatever. You couldn't do that. The work had to be independent of all ideologies, and the result could take many forms. My work, in practice, developed from treading the boards. So there's a weird autodidactic aspect to everything I've done, but it was driven by a feeling for what worked with an audience, which came out of the discipline and experience of live work. It wasn't primarily driven by theoretical concerns, though I was passionate about ideas. But I was also passionately dedicated to figuring out what really, actually communicates with the punters. That was my drive.

For the same reasons I went everywhere that I could with *Thriller,* and later with *The Gold Diggers* and with *Orlando.* I traveled the globe with the films and sat in the back of innumerable screenings, long beyond the point of aching boredom with my own work. Not to look at the work but to look at the audience, to look at the backs of their heads, to hear where they listen, where they cough, and see where they shuffle. Or to look at the walkouts or get things thrown at me in the case of *The Gold Diggers.* Or have people fall into my arms weeping at the end of other films, as has often been the case with *YES.* So I feel like they're my teacher, my audience, and I really mean that. I don't necessarily want to agree with them, but I want to find out how it all works.

CF: What kind of pleasures do you think your films give?

SP: I have observed the effect of my films on different audiences, in different places and at different times, and each film has given different pleasures. But the one that seemed to give the most all-round pleasure was *Orlando.* It really cut through all over the place. Partly because people laughed a lot, and there was irony in it, wit that seemed to work, and there's also a lot of visual splendor and color. Of course, it was put together over a very long period of time with a great deal of care compared to the earlier things I had done, and with more resources, which created a fuller, more polished "look." But *The Tango Lesson* seemed to give some people a different kind of pleasure. People still come up to me in the street in different countries, or write to me about it. But pleasure, you know, it's like using the word "entertainment," or "beauty" . . .

CF: Would you like me to use the word "entertainment"?

SP: Yes, because I think pleasure is a complicated word in the way that I would use it, let alone all of its meanings now, given all of the theoretical writing about the word. But a pleasurable cinematic experience can also be, perhaps, a very uncomfortable one, or an uneasy one. Pleasure is not necessarily the same as comfort, security, or happiness. Entertainment, similarly, doesn't necessarily mean levity. It can be something extremely serious, but maybe what's relaxing about entertainment at its best is that something has been worked through and crafted in such a way that there is no impediment to the experience. There is no obstacle. And that's what the release of entertainment is. It's like being swept up in skill, which creates the pleasurable feeling of clarity. But skill is quite a complex word, too.

CF: When I saw *Jerk* and *Hors d'oeuvres*, I was thinking about the way that, in those films, there really is a sense of experimentation. Thinking for the moment about the trajectory of your work, where does that sense of experimentation go once the longer length and, equally, narrative come in as a priority?

SP: I think experimentation takes many forms. Sometimes it's more subtle and hidden, but when the concern is with form itself, that's when the experimentation is more obvious, more visible. Actually I'm not sure I'd use the word "experimentation," I think I'd use the word "exploration" or "playfulness" or "questioning": not taking things for granted. But the bigger the budget, the more difficult it is to freely try different ways of making things and to take risks.

CF: Is that because you have to go by the script?

SP: The bigger the budget, the more you're locked in to both a schedule and the script: you're being watched, people are commenting on what you do as you do it. So from that point of view, a bigger budget gives you a bigger crew and apparently more resources and the ability to do things. But you're squeezed, intellectually squeezed. A lower budget is a terrible struggle, and you lack the material means of doing things, but you can be much freer, which makes it possible to take more risks and to be more flexible. For example, with *YES* I was able take a script as far as I could and then treat it as a kind of skin that gradually gets shed successively during a shoot and during the edit so that in effect, the writing process continues through to the very last moment of the editing. Whereas with *The Man Who Cried* I was locked into the script as it had manifested just before the shoot. It was a very large budget, but I had to cut twenty-six scenes in the week before the shoot and wasn't able to repair the damage, so I wasn't happy with what happened.

CF: There seems to be a moment in your cinema where something shifts, so you have *Thriller, The Gold Diggers,* that have been engaged with theoretical terms and are both in black and white. But then you have *Orlando,* which, as you say, is all color and aesthetic beauty. Are you aware of the moment?

SP: No, but I think the reason for the shift is slightly different. I love black and white. I find it very beautiful. I find minimalism beautiful. I can watch *Ten* [dir. Abbas Kiarostami; France/Iran, 2002], for example, filmed with just two video cameras in a car, and find the simplicity of the shape of that extremely beautiful; then watch a very, very slow [Alexandr] Sokurov film alongside six other people in the audience in the cinema and weep at its beauty. So beauty for me doesn't necessarily mean lots of color and fast-moving images. But I had a very strong experience with *The Gold Diggers,* because I was really slaughtered by most of the mainstream critics at the time, and afterwards it was extremely difficult for me to get to make another film.

It felt like a matter of life and death. I wanted more than anything to be a filmmaker, but nobody would give me a penny to make anything. I can't tell you the numbers of meetings, the numbers of rejections, the numbers of drafts, the numbers of doors that I knocked on and was turned away. I thought, "I've been slaughtered. How am I ever going to get up off this battlefield?" And also, "What can I learn from what I've done?" When I traveled with *The Gold Diggers,* one of the things that I learned was that perhaps it was hemmed in by its own critical/political concerns. Post-*Thriller,* I had maybe become too theoretically driven myself and influenced by what people had said to me about my work rather than working in a more intuitive way. I think that was one aspect of it.

Another was that I was driven with *The Gold Diggers* to make a strong political, feminist statement in the means of production, by having an all-female crew. Unfortunately, this turned out be an inexperienced and sometimes mutineering crew. So whereas now a starting-out director would surround himself or herself with an experienced crew, a good script editor, a producer who helps you in this and that and the other, I had a bunch of mates who wanted to kill me for being a director at all. I really hoisted myself on my own political petard, I would say, and suffered for it, so I made a decision not to do any more films that way.

CF: With Julie Christie, what kind of star image do you think she brought to that film at that moment?

SP: Well she's an icon, a British icon, and an international movie star. She has a face with proportions that are truly classical and a presence that is truly cinematic, and is therefore etched in an international consciousness. So she brought the value of all that with her into the film, the meaning of being a star in her particular blonde way at that moment. For me it was a deliberate, conscious attempt to have a star in a film where you wouldn't expect her to be, in a story that was about the deconstruction of the value of the star system, and of the industry itself, and an economic system based on the profit motive. So we were taking on the big ideas and using her luminous presence to both be inside and outside the star system.

CF: I guess in terms of independent cinema at that moment, nobody had ever placed a star within their frame or used the image in that way, had they?

SP: No. It refers back to what we were discussing earlier. I always wanted to see the films I made, however small they were, as part of the totality of cinema. And having Julie Christie in a film was part of that bridge-making process, where the impenetrable shininess of Hollywood could be demystified, decoded, broken into, opened up, talked to by another way of thinking. Or the other way of thinking could talk to it. I think it was a first. Now, of course, stars in independent film are ten a penny, but it really was groundbreaking at the time to do that. And groundbreaking of *her* to do that; it was a great act of courage on her part.

However, some of the critics couldn't resist asking, "What's Julie Christie doing in this film, when this director doesn't know how to make a film, she doesn't know how to tell a story?" There was no understanding of the fact that the structure was deliberately critical, deliberately cyclical, and was deliberately unresolved. Everything that it was, everything that it reached for, was trivialized by those critics and described as incompetence, which it was not. These were aesthetic decisions that were purposefully made.

However, it is true that I did not have my hands on my craft in the same way as I did have by the time I made *Orlando*. I started writing *Orlando* the day after I finished *The Gold Diggers*. I knew that I wanted to make an adaptation from the existing work, in color, and pace things in a faster way, less starkly meditative. These were lessons that the audience had taught me. And I wanted to find a way of being more subtle with my structural concerns, more universal with my political concerns, less didactic, less conceptual, but with a strong conceptual underpinning as a subtext. So my strategies clarified and gelled and eventually found form with *Orlando,* after a big struggle.

CF: You've mentioned Christie's classical film-star face, but that iconic way of filming women is something we also encounter in your other films. With a lot of your lead female characters, it is the face that you focus on. I just wondered if there's a system there about how you represent your females. Are you aware of focusing in this way?

SP: I focus on what is communicated by the whole body in wider shots, and what happens in the face as soon as there's a close-up. So then, really, it's more about how the close-ups are constructed and lit. In the case of both *Orlando* and *YES*, the director of photography was [Alexei] Rodionov, who does exquisite portrait lighting, and with *The Man Who Cried*, it was Sacha Vierny, who comes out of a not-dissimilar lighting tradition. But yes, I do have a great, great interest in the actor's face and spend a lot of time working on finding the right angle and frame and light for both the male and the female face, because the face is where we read things. The face is part of the body, but it's a very particular part of the body. And it is in many ways the portal into both thought and feeling. But I wouldn't say that how I film it is part of a *system* of representation. It's more within the tradition of much, much earlier Russian and Hollywood film. Both Griffith and Eisenstein put a huge amount of aesthetic energy into the power of the face. A close-up is an iconic way of framing and can be a very telling moment in a film. However, more important to me than the simple fact that it is a face, is what am I asking the actor to do when they're in that close-up? It's about trying to achieve a state of nakedness on the screen. Technically, that takes a lot of lighting, use of reflectors, and make-up, and hair, and all the rest, in addition to the actor's work. But above all it's the state of being in relation to the camera, a state of transparency, a state of consciousness beyond thought, trying to access the interior world without obstacle. That is the most important thing of all. A lot of work goes on between me and the actor to achieve that quality—some silent, some spoken. It's about attention to detail and attention to the person.

CF: And what about your male stars and your male characters. Do you work with them differently?

SP: No, in exactly the same way, an actor is an actor, whether male or female. And the needs of an actor are individual—they're similar and they're different, but the differences are individual ones, I think, rather than gender ones on the whole. The reality of a shoot, especially with people who aren't in the main role, is that the amount of time you spend with an actor is really very, very short in the overall process of development of the film. But the significance of the actor on the screen is huge. So there is an intensity to the contact, even if it's only for a few days.

For example, Billy Zane in *Orlando* was probably only shooting for a week, maybe less, and we had only a day or two of preparation. But what took the time was choosing him in the first place. So the casting process is crucial. And then the process of working with an actor once you're on the set is profoundly intimate. It's about building a relationship, in my case, anyway. I don't know how other directors work, but it is so central to what I do because the trust the actor places in you is the context for what they're able to do in front of the camera.

CF: Apart from your cameo actors George Yiasoumi and Lol Coxhill, you don't seem to have often worked more than once with people. Are there any actors you've worked with that you would want to work with again?

SP: Oh, quite a few, yes, I'd love to. I don't know why it hasn't happened. Perhaps people's lives diverge, or you create a role that you have to find a new fit for. But probably, if I was turning over more films more quickly, I would work with the same people again. I've had very good, even wonderful experiences on the whole with the actors I've worked with. I respect and adore them. And I think I've been helped by having had a background in performance myself, so I can both be very empathetic towards them, very respectful of the actors' process, and very interested in it.

CF: Could you ever see yourself going back to short films, the more experimental work? Given the constant difficulties involved in getting money for film art, there are quite a few filmmakers now who put their work in galleries. So is that something that you could see yourself doing?

SP: I've been asked to do things in galleries, but it's not really my universe. What's attractive about the world of fine art is that there is a certain permission for daring in the aesthetic and a certain kind of sophistication in the self-selecting audience that goes to a gallery that makes it possible to take certain formal risks. But one can do that on a film too. *YES* started life as a five-minute short, which I used as a pilot or an experiment to see if the idea was going to work. In fact, the original idea for *YES* was very much a return to roots and was made for a nothing kind of a budget. I think to survive as an independent filmmaker you have to be incredibly flexible both with budgets and ways of working. And it's interesting to be able to move flexibly within different levels of budget and see what's possible. But once you've made something that's gone out to millions of people, it's very hard to step down from that sense of the magnitude of an audience.

CF: Is there a kind of filmmaking with which you aligned yourself as you developed? Do you see like-minded directors?

SP: Yes, but they're not necessarily alive. Where I wanted to place myself was in the lineage of my heroes and teachers, such as Godard and Eisenstein. I always felt the *whole* of cinema was my history, and I wasn't going to take just that female bit, thank you very much, just as the whole of literature belongs to all writers. I experienced it as an enforced ghettoization, this identification with other filmmakers only by virtue of gender and with only certain subjects considered possible. I didn't want to make films about knitting, I didn't want to make films about children, I didn't want to make films about the female gaze. Or I might, but I didn't want to *have* to. I wanted to make films about maths, or global politics, or anything else I was interested in. That's the sort of feeling I always aimed for: that the world is my canvas, or the whole of world cinema is ours too. My struggle as a woman was to own that. Now I would identify more with some of the younger generation's work, like Lynne Ramsay's. I can see that she's working in the same zone.

CF: I suppose the reception of her work has been quite curious in a way because it hasn't been gendered.

SP: Because she's not in that first generation. With *The Gold Diggers,* I believe I was the first woman to direct a feature film since the fifties. First through the gate, the hoards trample on you as they steam past you.

CF: Or define themselves against you.

SP: Exactly. Each generation stands on the shoulders of the generation before. And I was aware, when younger, of standing on the shoulders of Dorothy Arzner, for example. I'm not sure how much Lynne Ramsey or indeed Sofia Coppola is aware of standing on my shoulders, but in parenthesis, I've noticed their work never gets called feminist, even though they have made very large parts for females, and they are women. Instead, Lynne has been embraced as a British filmmaker, so "feminist" is perhaps a generational label.

Jane Campion and myself always get called feminist filmmakers, even when there's a huge part for a man or when it's clear that there are multiple points of reference inside the work. So it's actually a label of age rather than of content and form. But the younger generation are now just called filmmakers, and that was always my dream. I dreamed of the day when somebody would just describe me as a filmmaker and not as a female filmmaker or a feminist filmmaker or attach a label that meant that I was still an outsider. And they've achieved that by virtue of being the next generation, which is great. But now I think we need to get given the gift back.

CF: I think there's also a difference of context there. There is a wider body of independent cinema now, so they can slip into that rather than being half "avant-garde" or "women's."

SP: It would be impossible for them to imagine what it was like for women in my generation growing up, the kinds of things that got said. When I first said I want to be a filmmaker, I was told, "Oh, everyone wants to be in the movies, dear," or, "You know, there are no women filmmakers." There was this sense of busting through an invisible wall, and the imaginative leap to say it is possible is a leap younger women don't have to make. They know it's possible because they've seen it. I remember Jane Campion saying to me that when younger women filmmakers are interviewed in Australia, the question is always asked: "Were you influenced by Jane Campion?" and they all go "No!" and she says, laughing, "Ungrateful brats." And you know it's a joke, but it's also understandable.

CF: In Europe there seem to be far more examples of women being included as respected filmmakers and carving out a stable career. I'm thinking of Claire Denis, Chantal Akerman, or Diane Kurys as examples in France. So how far do you think your career has been inhibited by staying in the U.K.?

SP: I've never been given money for a feature by Channel Four or BBC. They've always refused everything I've proposed. My work has not really been principally funded from this country, despite money from the BFI and British Screen.

CF: Did you ever think of basing yourself elsewhere?

SP: Yes, I've many times thought of emigrating, partly because my main audience is not in the U.K. It's a part of it, but in terms of numbers, my audience is elsewhere, and the keenest fans too. But where to go? This is the question. I don't really know. And it's a very strange question, this thing called roots. What are they? Especially as I seem to often define myself against England and Englishness. Maybe I need that push and pull, maybe I need the harshness of the environment of the U.K. But I sometimes look back and ask myself, if I'd emigrated twenty years ago, might I have made double the number of films? Sometimes I really regret the sheer amount of time spent having my things rejected. It hasn't made any difference in terms of my writing, but I think it probably has made a difference in terms of just the turnaround of the projects.

But where would I go? If I went to America, would I have done any better? I don't know. Maybe, because I think in America there's much more of a culture of supporting ambition. In Britain, there's also always been a climate of anti-intellectualism, the feeling—sometimes stated—of "who does she think she is?" which goes along with a distrust of a cinema of ideas. Possibly I would have had more joy in France, which is more supportive of its cinema, but French is not my first language. I speak French-ish now but didn't when I was younger. So I don't know what the solution is. So I'm still here, at the moment.

CF: You say that there hasn't been the financial support for your films in Britain, but what about critical support? How aware are you and how important are the reviews and writing about your work?

SP: I don't know how aware I am. To be honest, I think I protect myself from it to quite some degree. At the beginning I used to read all the reviews, but I've stopped doing that. Because they really are the twin impostors, success and failure, and if you start jumping up and down with glee every time you have a fabulous review, does that mean you should slash your wrists every time you have a bad one? So in the end, what I do is I seek out people whose views I really respect—not necessarily critics—and get their opinions.

But I'm also very interested in personal letters that I get from people, or the one-on-one contact with individual members of the audience. I'm incredibly open to their feedback, and it's very rewarding when things take me by surprise. For example, if a student suddenly comes up to me all nervous and trembling and says, "You've been my role model, as a person who's held out for integrity." This kind of thing sometimes gets said, and it's very moving, in what has often felt like a lonely struggle.

CF: Since *Orlando,* there seems to have been a pattern of big film, smaller film, in your choice of projects.

SP: Yes, I think that's because the smaller or the larger budget offers you different things. One of my motivations for doing *The Man Who Cried,* which in the end was a twenty-million-dollar budget, was to work with a really big crew (although actually *Orlando*'s crew was enormous). And I wanted to see what it was like working in the belly of the beast. I wanted to get out of the margins. In practice, the film was less successful than *Orlando,* so the equation is not clear, but it was interesting to experience: difficult, but interesting. A small budget like *YES* is a financial agony, partly because of working on a hundred-percent deferment of fees—though many of my other films have been made on the same basis. It means just accepting living with debts for years and asking people to do favors all the time and not being able to pay your crew properly. It's difficult, but if you want final-cut freedom then it's necessary.

CF: You have been talking about deciding to make larger-budget movies, but how does the budget affect the form? When did you start thinking, actually, "I need more money because I want to tell a story?"

SP: With *Orlando,* because prior to that I was more interested in pulling stories apart, and "narrative" was a dirty word, to some degree. Conventional storytelling was really not what I was interested in. I was interested in image, time, situation, and performance. But *Orlando* was my great teaching tool. By the time we went into production, I had spent about seven years working on the script, studying, and rereading the book, and reading everything else Virginia Woolf and others had ever written about the book. I analyzed it, drew up charts, and tried endless things to understand her not-very-conventional narrative, and in the process I became extremely interested in the structures of storytelling. I've always read fiction and have always told stories, but not always linear ones.

Incidentally, I did the Robert McKee screenwriter's weekend course later on, after I'd already written my adaptation of *Orlando,* and was gratified to find that one of his key rules was never try and adapt Virginia Woolf. I'm sure that he would not hold to that any more, but I was told by many people at the time that nobody can ever, nobody will ever, nobody *should* ever try and adapt Virginia Woolf.

CF: I read an interview that Rose English gave about art on film in which she suggested that there's a general distrust of the visual arts manifesting in England's literary culture. Did you find this in the reception of *Orlando?* Was there a kind of a snobbism from the Woolf appreciators?

SP: The reactions to *Orlando* were overwhelmingly positive. I know there was the odd carping insult, but there was mainly a tidal wave of positive appreciation from the critics. The film was the most universally liked of everything that I've done. From a literary and cinematic point of view, I had put a really massive amount of work into trying to figure out what a respectful adaptation might consist of, so that any changes I made with *Orlando* were not made lightly. My reasons were checked and rechecked. I came to the conclusion that you have to be respectful, but not slavish, to a book, especially a great one, in order for it to live as an adaptation on film. I'm not very fond of most adaptations, frankly, which tend to be overly reverential. I found the slight preciousness surrounding Woolf an irritating preciousness. I didn't find that quality in her own work. I didn't think it was true to her. And the whole preciousness around the Bloomsbury set I started to find nauseating after a while, however much I liked the work. But I'm a massive fan of Virginia Woolf. I think she's a great revolutionary and a great, great writer. I didn't like all of her politics. But I did think that what she was doing as a writer was extraordinary.

I thought *Orlando* itself was an underestimated book, and she was doing different things in it than most people seemed to think. She was absolutely working in parallel with James Joyce in developing the stream of consciousness and exploding the form of the novel. She was also infinitely, nail-bitingly ironic about the class system and about history. She wouldn't have any of the history of England being described as kings and queens and great big houses and lawns. It was a satire of England's view of itself. But an adaptation is an adaptation; it's not the same thing as the book. The book is strong enough to withstand a film existing. It doesn't destroy the book in any way whatsoever. In fact, I'm pretty certain that the film has led people back to the book in many cases.

I allowed a lot of conventions in *Orlando* that I resisted as a serious avant-gardist before that. And I let myself off the hook, let myself out of the structuralist jail in a way, and decided that everything that ever existed in the history of cinema was mine to use if I chose. So I think there's a kind of release and playfulness in the film that I can see now when I look at it. It's as if a disapproving superego has gone. But I was also following in Virginia Woolf's footsteps. She plays ironically with love at first sight and the deliciousness of looking at the beautiful Russian princess who's dressed as a boy. So it's all play within play and irony within irony, mirrors and smoke, not unlike the structure of *Thriller,* so that's why I say it was a break with the earlier work, and yet in another way it was a translation into terms that seemed more obviously accessible.

CF: How does the creative process work for you?

SP: Something happens at the beginning: there is a choice made that feels like a leap into the void or off a precipice—whatever metaphor you choose to use—and it is magical. You start with nothing, and gradually the words appear on the page, and then there is something. And then after that it's rewriting, editing, pruning, shaping, and crafting.

CF: Which brings us to *The Tango Lesson.* How did that project develop, particularly as it comes after *Orlando,* when you are at this pinnacle. How easy was it to find something that you wanted to do after that moment?

SP: Really difficult, because I got taken up by the big American studios—bouquets in the hotel room, and all that kind of thing—and found the experience confusing. Suddenly I was somebody whose films would make money, it's as simple as that. I had become more visible and more accessible with a film that was at that time making money for some people, but not, incidentally, for me. So I got offered loads and loads of stuff and agonized over it. It was a crossroads moment, and I could have gone to America and started making studio films. But instead I started work on about seven scripts of my own.

Then *The Tango Lesson* crept up on me. It was a private passion that I didn't really think could ever be transformed into a film or integrated into my working film life. But it was a film that I needed to make, and that's how it happened. I had discovered an amazingly interesting world in the tango in Buenos Aires and in the first year hardly slept a wink, stayed up all night every night going round the clubs by myself, walking through dark long streets, putting on those shoes, and taking four, five, six lessons a day with the old tango maestros. It was an intoxicating experience.

So then I thought, "Maybe a little film," and then I thought, "Maybe a documentary—a very ironic documentary, with myself in it as a kind of clown finding her feet." I asked myself, "Should I be in it? Should I not be in it?" And then I realized that I needed to be in it because that was the motor that was driving the engine. It came from my own desire both to learn and to dance and to embody. So it was a form of reconciliation with my early experience as a dancer in my early twenties, with my performer self.

I was taken aback by the criticisms of narcissism by putting myself in *The Tango Lesson,* and criticism of my personal appearance, too. Like every female, I'm critical of my own appearance, but I wasn't expecting the hatred that came from some quarters, of daring to put myself as an older woman on the screen, as if it was a kind of affront. This wasn't a universal response, but the charge of narcissism really took me aback, although on some level I knew it would come. But it was so opposite to the experience of making the film, which was so raw and challenging . . . I felt vulnerable rather than vain. Anyway, I think it's boring to see the same types of bodies all the time on the screen. The male body does tend to get shown in all its glory from youth to old age, in a more expansive and interesting way than women are allowed. I find it interesting to see experience in a face, to see suffering in a face like Joan Allen's, for example.

CF: Those criticisms of "narcissism" seem to be missing the point as well.

SP: Yes. You merely have to have a broader frame of reference in the arts to know that the integration of the persona of the artist in the work as a vehicle of exploration of point of view is a sturdy tradition; it is not narcissistic, it's a way of exposing phoney transparency and objectivity. So if you want to explore subjectivity and point of view in a film, it's a very useful way of doing it. Of course, in *The Tango Lesson,* these accusations of narcissism are partly produced by the blurring of fiction and reality at the core of the film.

A lot of people didn't seem to realize the project was about fiction and truth and was asking the question, Which story is being told? And from whose point of view? We find out at the end of the film that the film my character is thinking of making is the film we have been watching all along—a film that has obviously been written and rehearsed—so the questions about truth and illusion in cinematic fiction are inherently there. But I didn't realize how literal the journalistic probe would be later on and how outraged some people would be that I couldn't tell them what was "true" and what wasn't "true" in the story. I tried to explain that I used lived experience as a laboratory and then transformed it in the writing. For example, of course I wrote Pablo's lines, but that doesn't mean that he didn't say certain things that were a bit similar at some point in the "real" trajectory.

But this whole definition of what's real and what's not real is fascinating. Of course, documentaries have now suddenly started taking center stage, but most people don't realize how much you construct a documentary. It takes one back to completely fundamental questions of art, truth, and representation, which is exactly what I wanted *The Tango Lesson* to do. But I didn't think it would be a cause of outrage; I thought it would be a cause of interest.

CF: And you being in the film focuses those questions even more.

SP: Absolutely, and like using my own name. Obviously that was something I discussed: should I, shouldn't I call myself Alice or something? But then I thought, if I do that, people will think it's really my story anyway, and I'm trying to disguise it. But that's my one regret. It might have been more interesting to use another name just to put that little bit more doubt into the equation about what—or whose—story was being told.

CF: I think of these last three films together, from *The Tango Lesson* onwards, as all concerned in different ways with identity and a sense of place and with how we find our identity and then how we express that in terms of art, singing, dancing. Where does that theme come from?

SP: Well, if I think of it in a completely personal way, my family background of atheist, anarchist outsiders makes you feel like an exile within your own land. Plus, I grew up in an area where there were real refugees and exiles from Nazi Germany, many of them friends of my parents. And I think that feeling for and empathy with the outsider or the underdog really shaped me in a very profound way, and I'm still working on it. As I have never felt the norm, therefore I understand what it feels like for other people to feel not like the norm either. In the case of *The Tango Lesson,* I guess I used that partly as a metaphor, and also because I found it interesting to figure out, well, hang on a minute, you know I'm a white English female, and I'm making a film about the tango, an art form that developed in Argentina, itself a great melting pot of influences and cultures. But what does it mean for me to be daring to make a film about their thing? I was afraid that I would get it wrong, so I did my research very, very carefully and respectfully, and I guess that was part of my motivation for putting in the story itself an exploration of difference between the two main characters—one within the culture being explored but outside the world of cinema, and one within the world of cinema but outside the Argentinean culture.

The use of the Jewish metaphor in there actually belonged to the next film, which I had already written, and that often happens. The concerns from one film kind of seep into another, or there is a little seedling of the next one in there. I think it's also because I have some feeling of responsibility as a filmmaker not to create an ending that's closed. I try somehow to end a film on a note of hope. As with *YES,* for example, which I started to write on September 12, 2001. It was a response to the global situation. I felt it a matter of urgency that I made something that was not just a personal reflection about difference and identity. I wanted to contribute something positive in the face of a global emergency where the turning of the other, in this case the Arabic world and Islam, into the enemy of the West and the parallel reverse dehumanization and hatred of America, both seemed to threaten mass destruction.

I felt, as somebody working with fiction, I could get inside this dynamic and create two characters from those opposing global places who could talk to each other rather than kill each other. The ending then took on a huge symbolic significance: I needed to create a feeling that the door wasn't closed, that it was possible for these two individuals—not as symbols, exactly, but inevitably carrying identifiable cultural baggage with them—to find some kind of mutual respect, some kind of embrace.

CF: So how easily did the money come after *The Tango Lesson?*

SP: Not easily. *Orlando* made quite a lot of money, as I said, for the distributors. And with *The Tango Lesson* nobody lost any money, but it wasn't as big a commercial success, although it too sold in more than forty countries—in Paris it was very well received and ran for two years in a cinema. Plus I have never gone over budget or over schedule on a film. But the reason my films have always been hard to finance is because the new subject that I choose each time seems to have an enormous element of risk. It never resembles a thing I did before from the financiers' point of view, so it's like climbing a mountain all over again. If after *Orlando* I had said I really want to do *Son of Orlando,* there would have been a twenty-million-dollar check in my hand within minutes, I'm sure, but instead I proposed *The Tango Lesson* and was asked, "Why do you have to perform in it, Sally? Why does it have to be black and white? And who ever wants to see anything about tango?" It seems to be what I'm attracted to: risk.

CF: It sounds like you have to start every film anew.

SP: Yes, which may be because there is something to learn there or something to explore. I'm just not interested in repeating myself consciously. It's been drawn to my attention that I *have* repeated myself, but that is not what I have set out to do.

CF: It's for your audience to find the commonality, isn't it, and for you to keep doing different things.

SP: I guess: I tend to travel, literally and metaphorically. It's partly because the space of cinema is international: that's what I learned early on when I traveled with my films. If I am sitting in a full cinema in Florence or Sydney or Hong Kong or Tokyo, and these people who are watching the work are laughing at the same jokes and know more about my work than the English critics do, what does this mean? It means, although I was born in England and I'm English, my audience is international. You have to make a film about what you know, but I don't necessarily know more about the street outside my window than I do about a street in Havana. It's the journey of the character I have to know about.

CF: You mention Havana, and of course that's the closing location for *YES*. To some extent, the ending in Cuba is a great surprise triggered only by the aunt's words in the final twenty minutes of the film, so how do you decide on your locations for a film?

SP: I usually run parallel notebooks; so I have the script with all the dialogues, and also I have character notes in this great big folder, what they think, what they feel, what they might do, what they might not do, and stuff about the back story. It never necessarily appears in the film, but it's background information for me and for the actors so that we all understand who these people are. Then I'll have another notebook that's a sort of brainstorming process, about possible locations, or color or shapes, or textures, or clothes, or cars, or whatever, as I build up a mosaic. I usually have the notebooks all over the floor and images over the walls when I'm working, on the basis that the more you brainstorm around something and the more freely you can let your mind rove, the more likely you are going to find more interesting solutions and hopefully move away from cliché.

CF: And do you find that as a filmmaker you have traveled more to help your films to travel more in their content?

SP: Well, the ultimate travel is the kind of mind travel. I have been on an awful lot of airplanes—too many—and covered a lot of turf, but there are also a lot of places I haven't been to. I haven't been to the continent of Africa, haven't been to China. But I have watched films about China, read about China, and thought about China. Maybe the ultimate exploration is how deep you go rather than how broad you go, and so the travel in a story can be an image for another kind of voyage that's happening within the character, or it can just also be a setting. The director's job is to hold all those threads to shape the totality of the vision, even if you are working through the medium of other people's work, in which they also need to feel *their* own freedom of expression and individuality too. But directing ultimately is the holding of the space, creating a feeling of unification in a very practical way.

CF: You are very involved in the music of all of your films, composing and singing and writing lyrics, but how do you work with the other composers, producers, and musicians?

SP: For *The Gold Diggers,* I wrote the lyrics, and Lindsay Cooper wrote the music. She had been a long-term collaborator, and we worked closely together. In the case of *Orlando,* I shaped the score, conceptually and practically, but was greatly helped by David Motion, who both composed and arranged. Some parts of the score were made by me singing on multitracks in the studio in the middle of the night in the middle of the sound mix because money had run out. With *The Tango Lesson,* I chose the tango music. It was the result of a huge amount of research in Argentina. I then constructed the connecting pieces using a method of working in the studio with musicians and editing the layers of music together. So my role in the music is a kind of responsibility for the construction and overall shape of a score in collaboration with musicians. I am particularly dependent on the collaboration of Fred Frith and his improvised guitar lines. But it's true that I have a much greater degree of detailed involvement with the music than most directors. It seems to be quite unusual.

In *The Man Who Cried,* the score was written by Osvaldo Golijov, who is a brilliant composer and arranger. The music was designed to be a player or character in its own right in the film. There is a sense in which all music is a form of organized intelligence that is nonverbal and therefore expresses aspects, nuances, or experience in quite different ways than image or dialogue. In *The Man Who Cried,* song is a huge articulating thread in the story, and it was intended to be even more than it turned out, as, sadly, some of the gypsy scenes got cut. One day maybe I'll do another cut of that film.

CF: Can you talk about why you wrote *YES* in verse?

SP: I started by doing a five-minute short, nominally for a different project that I'd been asked to do, but it became the scene that eventually ended up as the argument in the car park at the apex of the film. The original idea was to go right into the middle of an argument between two people: you know nothing about them, but they bring with them these two different global points of view. In fact, the scene got rewritten many times, but the core of it was very similar in that first five-minute short. With almost every screenplay I've written there has been a version of it, or sections of it, in verse that I then jettisoned. I had this feeling with *YES* that the moment had arrived: that there was something about verse that could liberate the characters to speak about big abstract metaphysical ideas—aging, death, war, religion, and so on—which it would be hard to do in so-called normal speech without sounding artificial. The whole script is either in iambic pentameter, ten syllables per line, or eight syllables per line. It never deviates, even when the people are using half a line or so each in a conversation, and on the page you see that it always rhymes, even when you don't hear it. The verse was a kind of holding structure that was really strict. I didn't allow myself to depart from it anywhere, ever.

Within the form I wanted to find freedom with the ideas and to take them as far as I could, to take them for a wild walk. I knew that it was a huge risk and very challenging, but I had a lot of fun with it as well. The original short was made with Fiona Shaw and Simon Abkarian. Fiona was hugely encouraging about the verse and was a joy to work with, but she didn't end up being in the film for a whole combination of different reasons. I went on to develop the idea into a feature, as I had a real feeling of urgency about the East-West dialogue—that I needed to contribute something positive based on love rather than on hate.

CF: Did you start writing it just before you filmed *The Man Who Cried?*

SP: No. *The Man Who Cried* was finished way before I started writing *YES*.

CF: Did you write the regional accents into your script?

SP: Yes. I love the beauty of the regions and the beauty of all these different kinds of speech, even the beauty of somebody saying "fucking this and fucking that and fucking the other." Swearing can be a kind of repetitive music. So I was very interested in the musicality of different kinds of speech patterns and accents. The direction to all the actors, however, was to try and naturalize the verse, not to be reverential about it or draw attention to the rhymes or feel that the form was precious in any way, although they weren't to change a word! Unless of course I found that they couldn't say something because of a problem in the writing, in which case I would try and rewrite to make it more sayable.

But the direction was always just to follow the sense as if it was the way everyone spoke, and I think that's when it's at its most successful, when it's really naturalized in that way.

CF: And how did you find Simon Abkarian?

SP: He came to audition for *The Man Who Cried* as one of the gypsies. He was very good, but it was a scene that was cut, sadly, so he didn't end up in the film. But I remembered him and brought him over to read and thought he was really great. So he was in from the beginning.

CF: At what stage did Joan Allen come into the project?

SP: A bit later. I went through quite a few different people to arrive at her, but once I had found her I was absolutely sure. The chemistry between her and Simon was really good, and they are both very generous, respectful, serious actors and used to the ensemble process, having both started out in the theater. Joan, of course, has had three Oscar nominations but doesn't carry with her the diva baggage, and that makes her very easy to work with. A joy, in fact. I also liked that fact that their looks were polarized. Joan started doing interesting things with the language and was ready for a very different kind of role than the roles that she has usually been given, so it was a breakout role for her, which is nice.

In the preview screening of *YES*, I had several people sobbing afterwards in my arms, including one woman from a Muslim background who said she had never seen people from her side of the world humanized on screen by a Western filmmaker before. I was very pleased with the reactions, and some of the first reviews in the States are among the best reviews I have ever had. And some of the worst. But one would expect it to be a film that divides people.

CF: And how did John Berger contribute?

SP: Well, John Berger wrote me a letter after he saw *The Tango Lesson*. We have become friends, and I love his work, and I love him as a person. I went to stay with him in the Haute Savoie when I had done the first early draft of *YES*, when it was still just sections of verse spoken by each individual character. I read it all out to him, as poems, as a kind of dry run. Then we worked on structuring it together. He read the subsequent drafts intermittently and gave me feedback at different stages. So he has been a kind of mentor, and I couldn't hope for a better one. I think he's a fantastic example of somebody who's gone on learning and growing and developing and being open and enormously productive.

CF: Before I saw *YES* I was thinking that I should ask you about digital technologies and how much they have touched upon your work, and obviously in *YES* you have these kind of slow and manipulated images, but other than that, do you ever see yourself making a film digitally?

SP: Well, first of all, both *The Man Who Cried* and *YES* used digital postproduction. I don't just mean the editing but the whole grading [color correction] process and treating of the image.

CF: And how is that different from analog filmmaking?

SP: Just doing a graded print at the lab is a zillion miles away. When a film is graded at the lab you sit there and you say, "I would like that bit red or that a bit darker, or that a bit lighter." Then you come back a few days later to look at the next print, and you say, "Well, that image needs to change again." But in this case I'm sitting in a room twelve hours a day for three weeks, working with a colorist on every single frame reconstructed or painted digitally, virtually, and quite subtly. But all the speed variations were done on film in the camera. We shot six frames per second and then stretched it to twenty-four frames. Then there are sections that were filmed digitally, all the video bits, the CCTV bits, the confession at the end, and some of the footage of Cuba I took when I was doing location recces in Cuba with my little digital camera. I explored the possibility of shooting the whole film digitally, did quite a lot of tests, in fact, but wasn't convinced that it was the right texture for the image throughout the film. But I'm sure I will make a film digitally one day now that I have discovered what you can do in postproduction digitally with the image if you generate it electronically. But *YES* was shot on Super 16mm and then digitized. At this point there is still more information on film as a recording medium. But when we started to explore what could be done with it at Digimages in Paris, we were all taken by surprise. It's a whole new area, and that's interesting.

Note: *Jerk* (1969) and *Play* (1970) can be viewed at the British Artists Film and Video Study Collection at the Central St. Martins College of Art and Design, London (www.studycollection.org.uk). *Hors d'oeuvres* is available for rental or viewing from Lux distribution, London (www.lux.org.uk).

Thriller (1979; Great Britain)
Production: Sally Potter, Arts Council of Great Britain
Director, screenplay, camera, editor: Sally Potter
Production assistants: Lindsay Cooper, Rose English
U.S. distribution: Women Make Movies (www.wmm.com)
U.K. distribution: BFI Collection (www.bfi.org.uk)
Script collaborator: Colette Laffont
Photography: Sally Potter
Rostrum photography: Arthur Johns, Cinefex
Still photography: Clive Barda, Christina Burron, Stuart Robinson, Donald
    Southern, Group Three
Musician (bassoon): Lindsay Cooper
Sound recording: Sally Potter
Cast: Colette Laffont (Mimi/Mimi), Rose English (Musetta/Mimi), Tony
    Gacon (the Artist), Vincent Meehan (the Artist)
Black and White
33 minutes

The Gold Diggers (1983; Great Britain)
Production: British Film Institute Production Board, Channel Four
Production supervisors: Nita Amy, Donna Grey
Production coordinator (Iceland): Kristin Olafsdóttir
Distribution: BFI Collection (www.bfi.org.uk)
Director: Sally Potter
Screenplay: Lindsay Cooper, Rose English, Sally Potter
Director of photography: Babette Mangolte

Editor: Sally Potter
Assistant editor: Rose English
Art director, costumes: Rose English
Music: Lindsay Cooper
Lyrics: Sally Potter
Choreography: Sally Potter
Cast: Julie Christie (Ruby), Colette Laffont (Celeste), Hilary Westlake
   (Ruby's Mother), David Gale (Expert), Tom Osborn (Expert's Assistant),
   Jacky Lansley (Tap Dancer), George Yiasoumi (Stage Manager), Siobhan
   Davies, Juliet Fisher, Maedee Dupres (Dancers in Dream), Marilyn Mazur
   (Drummer), Georgie Born, Lol Coxhill, Dave Holland (Musicians in
   Ballroom), Vigdis Hrefna Palsdóttir, Maria Pétursdottir Ridgewell, Lucy
   Bennett (Young Ruby)
Black and white
89 minutes

The London Story (1986; Great Britain)
Production: Sally Potter, British Film Institute, Channel Four
Producer: Nancy Vandenburgh, Jill Pack
U.S. distribution: Women Make Movies (www.wmm.com)
U.K. distribution: Lux (www.lux.org.uk)
Director: Sally Potter
Screenplay: Sally Potter
Lighting and camera: Belinda Parsons
Editor: Budge Tremlett
Music: From *Romeo and Juliet,* by Sergei Prokofiev
Cast: Jacky Lansley (Jack Winger), Lol Coxhill (Mr. Popper), George
   Yiasoumi ("The Door"), Arthur Fincham (the Minister), Dennis
   Greenwood (Ice Skater), Dermott Murnaghan (Newscaster)
Color
15 minutes

Orlando (1992; Great Britain, Russia, Italy, France, Netherlands)
Production: Adventure Pictures Limited, Lenfilm, Mikado Film, Rio, Sigma
   Films, British Screen, European Co-Production Fund (U.K.), European
   Script Fund, National Film Development Fund
Producer: Christopher Sheppard
Distribution: Artificial Eye
Director: Sally Potter
Screenplay: Sally Potter
Director of Photography: Alexei Rodionov
Editor: Hervé Schneid
Music: David Motion, Sally Potter

Cast: Tilda Swinton (Orlando), Billy Zane (Shelmerdine), Lothaire Blutheau (the Khan), John Wood (Archduke Harry), Charlotte Valandrey (Sasha), Heathcote Williams (Nick Greene/Publisher), Quentin Crisp (Queen Elizabeth I), Peter Eyre (Mr. Pope), Thom Hoffman (King William of Orange), Kathryn Hunter (Countess), Ned Sherrin (Mr. Addison), Jimmy Sommerville (Singer/Angel), Dudley Sutton (King James I), John Bott (Orlando's Father), Elaine Banham (Orlando's Mother), Anna Farnworth (Clorinda), Sara Mair-Thomas (Favilla), Anna Healy (Euphrosyne), Simon Russell-Beale (Earl of Moray), Matthew Sim (Lord Francis of Vere)
Color
93 minutes

The Tango Lesson (1997; Great Britain, France, Argentina, Japan, Germany)
Production: Adventure Pictures, OKCO Films, PIE, Nippon Film Development and Finance, Imagica, Pandora Filmproduktion, Sigma Films, Arts Council of England, European Co-Production Fund (U.K.), Sales Company, Eurimages Conseil de l'Europe, Medien-und Filmgesellschaft baden-Würtemberg, NPS Televisie, Stichting Co-Productiefonds Binnenlandse Omroep, National Lottery through the Arts Council of England
Producer: Christopher Sheppard
Distribution: blaq out
Director: Sally Potter
Screenplay: Sally Potter
Director of Photography: Robby Müller
Editor: Hervé Schneid
Music: Sally Potter, Fred Frith
Cast: Sally Potter (Sally), Pablo Veron (Pablo), Gustavo Naveira (Gustavo), Fabian Salas (Fabian), David Toole (Fashion Designer), Carolina Iotti (Pablo's Partner), Carlos Capello (Carlos), Peter Eyre (English Tango Fan), Heathcote Williams (Builder), Morgane Maugran (Red Model), Geraldine Maillet (Yellow Model), Katerina Mechera (Blue Model), George Yiassoumis (Photographer)
Color, Black and White
102 minutes

The Man Who Cried (2000; Great Britain, France)
Production: Gypsy Films Limited, Working Title Films, Adventure Pictures, StudioCanal, Universal Pictures
Producer: Christopher Sheppard
Executive Producers: Tim Bevan, Eric Fellnar
Distribution: Universal
Director: Sally Potter

Screenplay: Sally Potter
Director of Photography: Sacha Vierny
Editor: Hervé Schneid
Music Producer: Sally Potter
Cast: Christina Ricci (Suzie), Cate Blanchett (Lola), John Turturro (Dante Dominio), Johnny Depp (César), Harry Dean Stanton (Felix Perlman), Claudia Lander-Duke (Young Suzie), Oleg Yankovskiy (Father), Diana Hoddinott (Foster Mother), Richard Albrecht (Foster Father), Alan David (Welsh Teacher), Imogen Claire (Audition Mistress), Miriam Karlin (Madame Goldstein), Pablo Veron (Dancing Romany)
Color
100 minutes

YES (2005; USA, Great Britain)
Production: Greenestreet Films, U.K. Film Council, Adventure Pictures, Studio Fierberg, National Lottery
Producers: Christopher Sheppard, Andrew Fierberg
Distribution: Greenestreet Films, Sony Picture Classics
Director: Sally Potter
Screenplay: Sally Potter
Director of Photography: Aleksei Rodionov
Editor: Daniel Goddard
Music: Sally Potter, Fred Frith
Cast: Joan Allen (SHE), Simon Abkarian (HE), Sam Neill (Anthony), Shirley Henderson (Cleaner), Sheila Hancock (Aunt), Samantha Bond (Kate), Stephanie Leonidas (Grace), Gary Lewis (Billy), Wil Johnson (Virgil), Raymond Waring (Whizzer)
Color
100 minutes

Agnostinis, Valentina. "An Interview with Sally Potter." *Framework* 14 (April 1981): 47.

Andrew, Geoff. "Sense and Sensuality." *Time Out,* November 12–18, 1997, 25–26.

Armstrong, Richard. Review of *YES,* dir. Sally Potter. *Senses of Cinema* 39 (April–June 2006). Accessed April 26, 2008. www.sensesofcinema.com/contents/dvd/06/39/yes.html.

Auty, Martin. Review of *Thriller,* dir. Sally Potter. *Monthly Film Bulletin* 47.559 (August 1980): 166.

Barrett, Eileen. "Response: Decamping Sally Potter's *Orlando.*" In *Re: Reading, Re: Writing, Re: Teaching Virginia Woolf.* Ed. Eileen Barrett and Patricia Cramer. New York: Pace University Press, 1995. 197–99.

Barron, Saskia. "Celeste and Ruby Go Digging." *Stills* 12 (June–July 1984): 31–32.

———. "Iced Gold." *Time Out,* May 4–10, 1984, 14.

Berger, John, and Sally Potter. "Affirmative Actions." *Vertigo* 2.8 (Spring/Summer 2005): 27–29.

Boorman, John, Tom Luddy, David Thomson, and Walter Donohue, eds. *Projections: Film-Makers on Film-Making.* No. 4. London: Faber and Faber, 1995.

Bradshaw, Peter. Review of *YES,* dir. Sally Potter. *The Guardian,* August 5, 2005.

Cameron-Wilson, James. Review of *YES,* dir. Sally Potter. *Film Review* 660 (August 2005): 104.

Campbell, Duncan. "People Were More Afraid of the Poetry." *The Guardian,* July 29, 2005.

Canby, Vincent. "Witty, Pretty, Bold: A Real She-Man." *New York Times,* June 12, 1993, 12.

Capp, Rose. "Crocodile Tears: Sally Potter's *The Man Who Cried.*" *Senses of Cinema* 14 (June 2001). Accessed March 20, 2007. www.sensesofcinema.com/contents/01/14/man_who cried.html.

Carroll, Noel. "Language and Cinema: Preliminary Notes for a Theory of Verbal Images." *Millenium Film Journal* 10.11 (Autumn/Winter 1981): 186–217.

Catsoulis, Jeanette. "Just Say Yes: An Interview with Sally Potter." *Reverse Shot,* July 2005. Accessed March 20, 2007. www.reverseshot.com/legacy/summer05/sallypotter.html.

Catsoulis, Jeanette, with responses by James Crawford and Michael Joshua Rowin. "Man, Verse, Woman: Sally Potter's *YES.*" *Indiewire,* July 2005. Accessed March 20, 2007. www.indiewire.com/movies/movies_050621yes.html.

Caughie, Pamela L. *Virginia Woolf and Postmodernism: Literature in Quest and Question of Itself.* Urbana: University of Illinois Press, 1991.

Chaw, Walter. "Clarifying the Image: Sally Potter Reflects on Her Films." *filmfreakcentral,* July 3, 2005. Accessed April 27, 2008. http://filmfreakcentral.net/notes/spotterinterview.htm.

Ciecko, Anne. "Sally Potter: The Making of a British Woman Filmmaker." In *Fifty Contemporary Filmmakers.* Ed. Yvonne Tasker. London: Routledge, 2002. 272–79.

———. "Transgender, Transgenre, and the Transnational: Sally Potter's *Orlando.*" *Velvet Light Trap* 41 (Spring 1998): 19–34.

Citron, Michelle. "Women's Film Production: Going Mainstream." In *Female Spectators Looking at Film and Television.* Ed. E. Deirdre Pribram. London: Verso, 1988. 45–63.

Clarke, Eileen. Review of *The Tango Lesson,* dir. Sally Potter. *Entertainment Weekly,* June 12, 1998, 84.

Columpar, Corinn. "The Dancing Body: Sally Potter as a Feminist Auteure." In *Women Filmmakers: Refocusing.* Ed. Jacqueline Levitin, Judith Plessis, and Valérie Raoul. Vancouver: University of British Columbia Press, 2002. 108–16.

Conner Bennett, Kathryn. "The Gender Politics of Death: Three Formulations of *La Bohème* in Contemporary Cinema." *Journal of Popular Film and Television* 32.3 (October 2004): 110–21.

Cook, Pam. "Border Crossing: Women and Film in Context." In *Women and Film: A Sight and Sound Reader.* Ed. Pam Cook and Philip Dodd. Philadelphia: Temple University Press, 1993. ix–xxiii.

———. "British Independents: *The Gold Diggers.*" *Framework,* April 24, 1984, 12–30.

———. Review of *The Gold Diggers,* dir. Sally Potter. *Monthly Film Bulletin* 604 (May 1984): 140–41.

Copjec, Joan. "*Thriller:* An Intrigue of Identification." *Cine-tracts* 3.3 (Fall 1980): 33–38.

Corliss, Richard. "A Film of One's Own." *Time,* June 7, 1993, 63.

Craft-Fairchild, Catherine. "Same Person . . . Just a Different Sex: Sally Potter's Construction of Gender in *Orlando.*" *Woolf Studies Annual* 7 (2001): 23–48.

Cummins, June. "What Are They Really Afraid Of? Repression, Anxiety, and Lesbian Subtext in the Cultural Reception of Sally Potter's *Orlando.*" In *Virginia Woolf and Her Influences: Selected Papers from the Seventh Annual Conference on Virginia Woolf.* Ed. Laura Davis, Jeanette McVicker, and Jeanne Dubino. New York: Pace University Press, 1998. 20–25.

Dargis, Manhola. "Sally Potter: A Director Not Afraid of Virginia Woolf." *Interview* 23.6 (June 1993): 42–43.

Degli-Esposti, Cristina. "Sally Potter's *Orlando* and the Neo-Baroque Scopic Regime." *Cinema Journal* 36.1 (Autumn 1996): 75–93.

De Lauretis, Teresa. *Alice Doesn't: Feminism, Semiotics, Cinema.* London: Macmillan Press, 1984.

Del Rio, Elena. "Rethinking Feminist Film Theory: Counter-Narcissistic Performance in Sally Potter's *Thriller.*" *Quarterly Review of Film and Video* 21.1 (January 2004): 11–24.

Dixon, Wheeler Winston. *It Looks at You: The Returned Gaze of Cinema.* Albany: State University of New York Press, 1995.

Dobson, Patricia. Review of *Orlando,* dir. Sally Potter. *Screen International* 853. (April 1992): 23.

Donohue, Walter. "Against Crawling Realism: Sally Potter on *Orlando.*" In *Women and Film: A Sight and Sound Reader.* Ed. Pam Cook and Philip Dodd. Philadelphia: Temple University Press, 1993. 216–25.

———. "Immortal Longing: Walter Donohue Talks with Sally Potter." *Sight and Sound* 3.3 (March 1993): 10–12.

Dowell, Pat. "Demystifying Traditional Notions of Gender: An Interview with Sally Potter." *Cinéaste* 20.1 (Winter 1993): 18–21.

D'Silva, Beverley. "Shall We Dance?" *The Guardian,* October 27, 1997, 7.

Dunford, Mike. "Four Statements" (1976). Unpublished Artist's Statement. British Artists' Film and Video Collection, London.

Ehrenstein, David. *Film: The Front Line.* Denver: Arden Press, 1985.

———. "Out of the Wilderness: An Interview with Sally Potter." *Film Quarterly* 47.1 (October 1993): 2–7.

———. Review of *Orlando,* dir. Sally Potter. *The Advocate* 630 (June 1, 1993): 71–73.

Elwes, Catherine. "On Performance and Performativity: Women Artists and Their Critics." *Third Text* 18.2 (March 2004): 193–97.

Feay, Suzi. "Woolf Whistles." *Time Out,* March 10–16, 1993, 16–18.

Felperin, Leslie. Review of *YES,* dir. Sally Potter. *Sight and Sound* 15.8 (August 2005): 83–84.

Ferriss, Suzanne, and Kathleen Waites. "Unclothing Gender: The Postmodern Sensibility in Sally Potter's *Orlando.*" *Literature-Film Quarterly* 27.2 (April 1999): 110–16.

Finney, Angus. "Case Study: *Orlando.*" In *A Dose of Reality: The State of European Cinema.* London: Screen International, 1994. 92–96.

Fischer, Lucy. "Dancing through the Minefield: Passion, Pedagogy, Politics, and Production in *The Tango Lesson.*" *Cinema Journal* 43.3 (Spring 2004): 42–58.

Florence, Penny. "Debate: A Conversation with Sally Potter." *Screen* 34.3 (October 1993): 275–84.

Foundas, Scott. Review of *YES*, dir. Sally Potter. *Variety*, September 20, 2004, 61–62.

Fowler, Catherine. "Cinefeminism in Its Middle Ages, or 'Please, Please, Please Give Me Back My Pleasure': The 1990s Work of Sally Potter, Chantal Akerman, and Yvonne Rainer." In *Women Filmmakers: Refocusing.* Ed. Jacqueline Levitin, Judith Plessis, and Valérie Raoul. Vancouver: University of British Columbia Press, 2002. 51–61.

Francke, Lizzie. Review of *Orlando,* dir. Sally Potter. *Sight and Sound* 3.3 (March 1993): 48.

French, Philip. "Romance in Rhyme." *The Observer,* August 7, 2005.

Garrett, Roberta. "Costume Drama and Counter Memory: Sally Potter's *Orlando.*" In *Postmodern Subjects/Postmodern Texts.* Ed. Jane Dowson and Steven Earnshaw. Amsterdam: Rodopi, 1995. 89–99.

Gerard, Raymond. "Shall She Dance?" *Village Voice,* November 18, 1997, 82.

Glaessner, Verina. "Fire and Ice." *Sight and Sound* 2.4 (August 1992): 12–15.

———. "Interviews with Three Women Filmmakers." *Time Out,* March 17–23, 1972, 46.

———. "Sally Potter." *Cinema Rising* 1 (April 1972): 8.

Goldberg, RoseLee. *Performance: Live Art since the 1960s.* London: Thames and Hudson, 1998.

Goodman, Lizbeth. "Subverting Images of the Female (Interview with Tilda Swinton)." *New Theatre Quarterly* 6.23 (August 1990): 215–28.

Guano, Emanuela. "She Looks at Him with the Eyes of a Camera: Female Visual Pleasures and the Polemic with Fetishism in Sally Potter's *The Tango Lesson.*" *Third Text* 18.5 (September 2004): 461–74.

Hankins, Leslie K. "Redirections: Challenging the Class Axe and Lesbian Erasure in Potter's *Orlando.*" In *Re: Reading, Re: Writing, Re: Teaching Virginia Woolf.* Ed. Eileen Barrett and Patricia Cramer. New York: Pace University Press, 1995. 168–84.

Hibbin, Sally. Review of *The Gold Diggers,* dir. Sally Potter. *Films and Filming* 357 (June 1984): 15.

Hill, John. *British Cinema in the 1980s.* Oxford: Oxford University Press, 1999.

Hoberman, J. "Truth of Beauty." *Village Voice,* November 18, 1997, 82.

———. "Woolf in Potter's Clothing." *Premiere* 6.11 (July 1993): 43–45.

Hodges, Adrian. "BFI Backs *Gold Diggers'* All-Women Production Team." *Screen International* 346 (June 1982): 11.

Hollinger, Karen, and Teresa Winterhalter. "Orlando's Sister, or Sally Potter

Does Virginia Woolf in a Voice of Her Own." *Style* 35.2 (Summer 2001): 237–61.

Hoyle, Brian. "Intertextuality and Film: Sally Potter's *Orlando.*" In *European Intertexts: Women's Writing in English in a European Context.* Ed. Patsy Stoneman, Ana Maria Sànchez-Arce, and Angela Leighton. Bern, Switz.: Peter Lang, 2005. 193–214.

Humm, Maggie. "Postmodernism and *Orlando.*" In *Feminism and Film.* Bloomington: Indiana University Press, 1997. 142–78.

Imre, Aniko. "Twin Pleasures of Feminism: *Orlando* Meets My Twentieth Century." *Camera Obscura* 18.3 (December 2003): 176–211.

Indiana, Gary. "Spirits Either Sex Assume." *Artforum International* 31.10 (Summer 1993): 88–92.

Johnston, Andrew. Review of *The Man Who Cried,* dir. Sally Potter. *US Weekly,* June 11, 2001, 88.

Johnston, Claire. "Women's Cinema as Counter-Cinema." In *Screen Pamphlet: Notes on Women's Cinema,* No. 2. Society for Education in Film and Television, 1972. 24–31.

Johnston, Sheila. "Like Night and Day." *Monthly Film Bulletin* 51.604 (May 1984): 141–42.

Kaplan, E. Ann. "Night at the Opera: Investigating the Heroine in Sally Potter's *Thriller.*" *Millennium Film Journal* 10.11 (Fall 1981–Winter 1982): 115–22.
———. *Women and Film: Both Sides of the Camera.* New York: Methuen, 1983.

Kenny, Glenn. Review of *YES,* dir. Sally Potter. *Premiere* 18.9 (June 2005): 56.

Kuhn, Annette. *Women's Pictures: Feminism and Cinema.* 1982; reprint, London: Verso, 1994.

Lane, Christina. "The Compromised Sexual Positioning of *Orlando:* Postmodern Play in Gender and Filmic Conventions." *Australian Screen Education* 31 (Autumn 2003): 95–98.

Lanouette, Jennine. "Potter's Yield." *Premiere* 6.11 (July 1993): 80–81.

Lord, Catherine. "Becoming Still, Still Moving: Theoretical Pleasure in Sally Potter's *Orlando.*" In *Discern(e)ments: Deleuzian Aesthetics/Esthétiques Deleuziennes.* Ed. Joost De Bloois, Sjef Houppermans, and Frans-Willem Korsten. Amsterdam: Rodopi, 2004. 171–85.

Lucas, Rose. "*Orlando.*" In *The Cinema of Britain and Ireland.* Ed. Brian McFarlane. London: Wallflower Press, 2005. 217–26.

Lucia, Cynthia. "Saying 'Yes' to Taking Risks: An Interview with Sally Potter." *Cineaste* 30.4 (Fall 2005): 24–31.

MacDonald, Scott. *A Critical Cinema: Interviews with Independent Filmmakers.* Berkeley: University of California Press, 1998. 397–427.
———. "Interview with Sally Potter." *Camera Obscura* 10.35 (May 1995): 186–221.

MacRitchie, Lynn. *About Time: Video, Performance, and Installation by Twenty-One Women Artists.* London: Institute of the Contemporary Arts, 1980.

———. "Art on Film/Film on Art." In *Live Art Now Performance.* 28–29.

Malcolm, Derek. "Light and Liberty." *The Guardian,* March 11, 1993.

Marcus, Jane. Review of *Orlando,* dir. Sally Potter. *Women's Review of Books* 11.4 (January 1994): 11–12.

Maslin, Janet. "Julie Christie in *Gold Diggers* from Britain." *New York Times,* February 12, 1988, 18.

———. Review of *The Tango Lesson,* dir. Sally Potter. *New York Times,* November 14, 1997, 20.

McFarlane, Brian. Interview with Sally Potter. In *An Autobiography of British Cinema by the Actors and Filmmakers Who Made It.* London: Methuen, 1997. 456–561.

McKim, Kristi. "'A State of Loving Detachment': Sally Potter's Impassioned and Intellectual Cinema" (Great Directors Entry). *Senses of Cinema.* Accessed March 20, 2007. www.sensesofcinema.com/contents/directors/06/potter.html.

Mellencamp, Patricia. "Taking a Clue from Ariadne." In *Indiscretions: Avant-Garde Film, Video, and Feminism.* Bloomington: Indiana University Press, 1990. 149–72.

———. "What Virginia Woolf Did Tell Sally Potter." In *A Fine Romance: Five Ages of Film Feminism.* Ed. Patricia Mellencamp. Philadelphia: Temple University Press, 1995. 281–90.

Mitchell, Elvis. Review of *The Man Who Cried,* dir. Sally Potter. *New York Times,* May 25, 2001.

Monk, Claire. Review of *The Tango Lesson,* dir. Sally Potter. *Sight and Sound* 7.12 (December 1997): 54–55.

Moore, Madeline. "Virginia Woolf and Sally Potter: The Play of Opposites and the Modern Mind in *Orlando.*" In *Re: Reading, Re: Writing, Re: Teaching Virginia Woolf.* Ed. Eileen Barrett and Patricia Cramer. New York: Pace University Press, 1995. 184–97.

Moore, Suzanne. "Here's Looking at You, Kid!" In *The Female Gaze: Women as Viewers of Popular Culture.* Ed. Lorraine Gamman and Margaret Marshment. London: Women's Press, 1988. 44–59.

Morgan, Robin. "Who's Afraid of Sally Potter? *Orlando,* Written and Directed by Sally Potter." *Ms.* 4.1 (July/August 1993): 78–79.

Mulvey, Laura. "Afterthoughts on 'Visual Pleasure and Narrative Cinema,' Inspired by King Vidor's *Duel in the Sun.* (1946)." *Framework* 15/16/17 (Summer 1981): 12–15.

———. "Visual Pleasure and Narrative Cinema." *Screen* 16.3 (Autumn 1975): 6–18.

Neville, Lucy. Review of *Orlando,* dir. Sally Potter. *Sight and Sound* 13.10 (October 2003): 76.

Oppenheimer, Jean. "Production Slate: A Cross-Cultural Romance" (Interview with Alexei Rodionov). *American Cinematographer* 86.7 (July 2005): 30, 32–33.

Parsons, Louise. "Digging for Gold: Lessons from Sally Potter's *The Gold Diggers.*" *N. Paradoxa: International Art Journal* 5 (January 2000): 5–12.

Pidduck, Julianne. "Travels with Sally Potter's *Orlando:* Gender, Narrative, Movement." *Screen* 38.2 (Summer 1997): 172–89.

Potter, Sally. "Application to Arts Council: Film Bursary." British Artists Film and Video Study Collection, London. 1977.

———. "Bruises and Blisters." *Sight and Sound* Supplement for the London Film Festival, November 1997, 4–5.

———. "*Gold Diggers* and Fellow Travellers: Introduction to Potter's Season of Films at the NFT, London." *Monthly Film Bulletin* 51.604 (May 1984): 141–42.

———. "Gotta Dance: *The Tango Lesson.*" In *Projections: Film-Makers on Film-Making.* No. 4. Ed. John Boorman, Tom Luddy, David Thomson, and Walter Donohoe. London: Faber and Faber, 1995. 291–98.

———. *The Man Who Cried.* London: Faber and Faber, 2000.

———. "On Shows." In *About Time: Video, Performance, and Installation by Twenty-One Women Artists.* Ed. Catherine Elwes, Rose Garrard, and Sandy Nairne. London: Institute of the Contemporary Arts, 1980.

———. "On Tour with *Orlando.*" In *Projections: Film-makers on Film-making.* No. 3. Ed. John Boorman and Walter Donohoe. London: Faber and Faber, 1994. 196–212.

———. *Orlando: The Screenplay.* London: Faber and Faber, 1994.

———. "Performance: On Shows." In *Framing Feminism: Art and the Women's Movement, 1970–1985.* Ed. Rozsika Parker and Griselda Pollock. London: Pandora, 1987. 290–92.

———. "Sally Potter on *Thriller.*" *Camera Obscura* 5.9 (Spring 1980): 98.

———. "There Will Now Be a Short Intermission." British Film Institute PB 31, Paper No. 3. June 6, 1973.

———. *YES: Screenplay and Notes.* New York: Newmarket Press, 2005.

Projansky, Sarah. *Watching Rape: Film and Television in Postfeminist Culture.* New York: New York University Press, 2001.

Rainer, Yvonne. "A Quasi Survey of Some 'Minimalist' Tendencies in the Qualitatively Minimal Dance Activity Midst the Plethora, or an Analysis of Trio A." In *Yvonne Rainer: Work, 1961–73.* Novia Scotia: Halifax Press of the Nova Scotia College of Art and Design, 1974. 63–69.

Review of *The London Story,* dir. Sally Potter. *City Limits* 320 (November 19, 1987): 26.

Rich, B. Ruby. "Femicide Investigation." In *Chick Flicks: Theories and Memories of the Feminist Movement.* Durham, N.C.: Duke University Press, 1998. 227–32.

————. "In the Name of Feminist Film Criticism." In *Issues in Feminist Film Criticism*. Ed. Patricia Erens. Bloomington: Indiana University Press, 1985. 268–87.

————. "Prologue: 'The Allure of Alchemy' and 'Femicide Investigation.'" In *Chick Flicks: Theories and Memories of the Feminist Movement*. Durham, N.C.: Duke University Press, 1998. 220–32.

Rosen, Leah. Review of *The Man Who Cried*, dir. Sally Potter. *People Weekly*, June 11, 2001, 35.

Rosenbaum, Jonathon. "*The Gold Diggers*: A Preview." *Camera Obscura* 12 (July 1984): 126–29.

Sarris, Andrew. "A World War Interrupts a Young Girl's Fairy Tale." *New York Observer*, June 4, 2001.

Shaugnessy, Nicola. "Is S/he or Isn't S/he? Screening *Orlando*." In *Pulping Fictions: Consuming Culture across the English/Media Divide*. Ed. Deborah Cartnell, I. Q. Hunter, H. Kaye, and Imelda Whelehan. London: Pluto Press,, 1996. 43–56.

Stokes, Peter. "Consuming Desires: Performing Gender in Virginia Woolf's *Orlando*, Neil Jordan's *The Crying Game*, and Sally Potter's *Orlando*." *Consumption, Markets, and Culture* 1.4. (1998): 303–423.

Swanson, Gillian, and Lucy Moy-Thomas. "An Interview with Sally Potter." *Undercut* 1 (March/April 1981): 41–44.

Taubin, Amy. "About Time." *Village Voice*, June 22, 1993, 62.

Thom, Rose Anne. Review of *The Tango Lesson*, dir. Sally Potter. *Dance Magazine* 71.12 (December 1997): 84–86.

Vincendeau, Ginette. Review of *The Man Who Cried*, dir. Sally Potter. *Sight and Sound* 11.1 (January 2001): 53–54.

Vollmer, Ulrike. "I Will Not Let You Go Unless You Teach Me the Tango: Sally Potter's *The Tango Lesson*." *Biblical Interpretation* 11.1 (January 2003): 98–112.

————. "Towards an Ethics of Seeing: Sally Potter's *The Tango Lesson*." *Literature and Theology* 19.1 (March 2005): 74–85.

Walter, Natasha. "Potter's Craft." *Vogue* 150 (December 1992): 31–32.

Watkins, Susan. "Sex Change and Media Change: From Woolf's to Potter's *Orlando*." *Mosaic* 31.3 (September 1998): 41–63.

Weinstock, Jane. "She Who Laughs First Laughs Last." *Camera Obscura* 5.9 (Spring 1980): 99–110.

West, Dennis, and Joan M. West. "Achieving a State of Limitlessness: An Interview with Tilda Swinton." *Cinéaste* 20.1 (Winter 1993): 18–21.

Winters, Laura. "Filming the Tango: The Intricate Steps of Life and Love." *New York Times*, November 16, 1997, 19.

Woolf, Virginia. *Orlando: A Biography*. 1928; reprint, London: Penguin Books, 2000.

———. *A Room of One's Own.* 1928; reprint, New York: Penguin Books, 2004.

Young, Deborah. Review of *The Man Who Cried,* dir. Sally Potter. *Variety* 380.5 (September 18, 2000): 37–38.

Zeig, Sande. "Queens of England." *Filmmaker* 1.4 (July 1993): 24–26.

Kaplan, E. Ann, 33, 40
Keane, Tina, 13
Kelly, Mary, 13
Kidron, Beeban, 3
Kristeva, Julia, 34
Kuhn, Annette, 34, 36

Laffont, Colette, in *Thriller,* 8, 32, 34, 35, 36
Lansley, Jacky, 21, 24, 56
Le Grice, Malcolm, 16; *Horror Film 1* (1971), 15
Lenfilm Studios, 57, 58
Limited Dance Company, 21, 112
literature: modernist, 8; poetic dialogue, in *YES,* 96–99; writers of, as influences on Potter, 4
London Filmmakers' Co-op, 111; and expanded cinema, 15; Potter joins, 12
London Story, The, 1, 56–58

Malcolm, Derek, 60
Man Who Cried, The, **89;** ending of, 5, 87–95; lack of success of, 3; production of, 115, 122
Marx brothers (comedians), 12, 23
Marx Brothers (musical group), 21
Maslin, Janet, 46
McCall, Anthony, 15
Mikado Film, 58
Mirrors: in *The Tango Lesson,* 80–81, 83; in *Thriller,* 40
Monk, Claire, 3
Moore, Suzanne, 81
Motion, David, 130
Mulvey, Laura: and Peter Wollen, 3, 45, 112; and *Visual Pleasure,* 48, 77
My Beautiful Launderette (Kureshi/ Frears), 45

narrative: and alternate ways of making meaning, 54–55, 88; circular, 65, 76; as circumscribing the actions of women, 7; and the coming together of the couple, 5; episodic, 10; as retelling and rewriting of stories, 34, 37, 39; and quests, 55

National Film Development Fund (NFDF), 58
Naveira, Gustavo, 82
Nicholson, Annabel, 13, 16; *Reel Time* (1973), 15

Orlando (Potter film): and adaptation, 123–24; ending of, 5; Orlando's look in, 31; and playing with gender roles, 43, 56–75, **65;** and theatrical effects, 2
Orlando (Woolf novel), 23; Potter's adaptation of, 61

Papaconstantinou, Letha, in *The Building,* 16
performance: as art, 9, 14; use of performers as well as actors, 8; distinguished from acting, 29; in film, 28; on- and offscreen, 11–22; by Potter, 12–13; proliferation of, 13; as put on in *Orlando,* 64, 68–69; and theatricalization, 32
Pidduck, Julianne, 60
Play, 1, 12, 14, **18;** description of, 17–18
pleasure: and deconstruction, in *Thriller* and *The Gold Diggers,* 10; desire for, in song lyric, 48; and movement away from antipleasure in *YES,* 96; in *Orlando,* 63; Potter on, 113–14; from seeking answers to questions, 5; from use of music, dance, and poetry, 5–6
point of view, 39–40
postmodern use of costume drama in *Orlando,* 60
Potter, Sally: biography of, 11–12, 109; and desire to please, 29; interests of and influences on, 4, 8, 111
Powell, Michael, 12, 57
Projections 4, and chapter on *The Tango Lesson,* 2, 86

Rainer, Yvonne: and *Film about a Woman Who . . .* (1974), 30; and Judson Dance Theater, 13; and *Lives of Performers* (1972)
Ramsay, Lynne, 3
Rhodes, Lis, 15; and *Light Reading,* 36
Ricci, Christina, 78

Catherine Fowler is a senior lecturer in film at the
University of Otago, New Zealand, the coeditor of
*Representing the Rural: Space, Place, and Identity in
Films about the Land,* and the editor of *The European
Cinema Reader.*

Books in the series Contemporary Film Directors

The University of Illinois Press
is a founding member of the
Association of American University Presses.

Composed in 10/13 New Caledonia
with Helvetica Neue display
by Jim Proefrock
at the University of Illinois Press
Manufactured by Sheridan Books. Inc.

University of Illinois Press
1325 South Oak Street
Champaign, IL 61820-6903
www.press.uillinois.edu